MANAGE YOUR
ONLINE REPUTATION

MANAGE YOUR ONLINE REPUTATION

Tony Wilson

Self-Counsel Press
(a division of)
International Self-Counsel Press Ltd.
USA   Canada

Self-Counsel Press acknowledges the financial support of the Government of Canada through the Canada Book Fund (CBF) for our publishing activities.

Printed in Canada.

First edition: 2011

Library and Archives Canada Cataloguing in Publication

Wilson, Tony
    Manage your online reputation / Tony Wilson.

ISBN 978-1-77040-056-6

1. Internet in public relations. 2. Internet in publicity.
3. Corporate image. 4. Personal information management.
5. Online identities. 6. Online social networks. I. Title.

HD59.2.W56 2010   659.20285'4678   C2010-902051-0

"Top Ten Mistakes Lawyers Make with Social Media" by Doug Cornelius on page 157 is used with permission.

Photograph of Tony Wilson by photographer Kent Kallberg (www.kallbergstudios.com) used with permission.

Every effort has been made to obtain permission for quoted material. If there is an omission or error, the author and publisher would be grateful to be so informed.

Mixed Sources
Product group from well-managed
forests, and other controlled sources
www.fsc.org Cert no. SW-COC-002358
© 1996 Forest Stewardship Council

Self-Counsel Press
(a division of)
International Self-Counsel Press Ltd.

1704 North State Street
Bellingham, WA 98225
USA

1481 Charlotte Road
North Vancouver, BC V7J 1H1
Canada

CONTENTS

NOTICE TO READERS

ACKNOWLEDGMENTS

The good people at Self-Counsel Press, who cajoled me over drinks to write this book, must be thanked for their patience, particularly Eileen Velthuis and Sarah Yu. When the original deadline for this book was missed, I reminded them of my favorite quote from the late Douglas Adams, who wrote *The Hitchhiker's Guide to the Galaxy*: "I love deadlines. I love the whooshing noise they make as they go by."

I had help from many people in this venture. First, I'd like to thank my children Emma and Jeremy Wilson, who taught me how Facebook works but who still refuse to "friend" me, despite the fact they'll "friend" my old friend Roger Barron, who I'd also like to thank for his input on the way "kids" use social media, and the way they shouldn't. I'd also like to thank my wife Mary-Jane for putting up with me during the book writing process. I'm no fun when there's a deadline I haven't met.

Michael Allabarton of BrandDig Consulting in Victoria must be thanked for his excellent input and advice on branding, both for this book, and for one of my columns that appeared in *The Globe and Mail*, and Samantha Wilson for her input on sexting and Internet safety for children. Thanks also go to Dr. Susan Biali and Aly Kanji for their input on early drafts.

I saw some excellent examples of what *not* to say or post on Facebook and other social media sites from people who probably don't want to be named. But thanks all the same. Your input was immeasurably helpful.

Last but not least, I had some excellent help in researching and preparing draft text on privacy and defamation from Heather Mathison, a Vancouver lawyer who offered her assistance to me (and whose help I gratefully accepted).

Any mistakes, however, although accurate at the time of writing, are purely my fault, but they'll be fixed soon. That's how fast things happen online.

INTRODUCTION:
DEATH BY FACEBOOK

Like many of the most interesting moments in life (literary and otherwise), the opportunity doesn't so much knock at the door as fall from the sky from nowhere, landing on your plate for you to either take advantage of or not. If you're really lucky, drinks may be involved.

I practice franchising, licensing, and intellectual property law in Vancouver, British Columbia. Although the bulk of my practice involves franchised restaurants, hotels, and retail businesses, a fair chunk of my legal practice involves trademarks, copyright, technology licensing, intellectual property, and privacy law, and all of these interesting areas of law involve, to some degree, the use or misuse of the Internet.

In September of 2009, I met with the managing editor and publicist of Self-Counsel Press at a warm outdoor patio bar (Cactus Club, if you must know), over a couple of bottles of Kim Crawford Pinot Noir to discuss the just-released second edition of *Buying a Franchise in Canada*. The first edition had sold out and we were about to release the second edition with new updates. It seemed like a good excuse for drinks with the managing editor and publicist!

I used this moment to pitch another book on franchise law but from a different perspective. Instead, the managing editor, Eileen Velthuis, pitched a book to me, which I can tell you, doesn't happen that much in the book business.

"We'd like you to write a book for us about online reputation management," Velthuis said. "The book would be about how to manage your personal reputation online as well as your company's brand and reputation over the Internet in this environment of Facebook, Twitter, LinkedIn, and YouTube. There are intellectual property issues, privacy issues, contract issues, and the whole area is very cutting edge. What do you think?"

I knew my own kids were on Facebook all of the time, but I wasn't "on it," and frankly, I didn't see the need or have the desire to reconnect with people who I could just as easily keep in contact with by emailing, sending a card by regular mail, or simply picking up the telephone and calling them. Or, of course, I could choose to avoid them altogether!

As for LinkedIn, I was "on it" but wasn't really using it for anything other than posting my biography and responding to others who wanted to be part of my business network. LinkedIn is a big online place for building up your résumé. If you're not in the job market, you might not use it as much as people who are (or who expect to be).

It was an interesting moment to have been pitched a book on something as "cutting edge" as online reputation management. I could have set my mind back to 1978, where, as a summer researcher for the British Columbia Government in Victoria, I was shown a new technological wonder where electronic copies of original documents could be sent from Victoria to Vancouver (or anywhere else in the world for that matter) over telephone lines using a machine about the size of a television set. It was called a Facs machine; facs standing for facsimile (which everyone wrote as "fax").

Or, I could have recalled 12 years later, a meeting at one of my old law firms where the partners regaled against this new system called "voice mail." Messages were not personally left with a receptionist and written on a small piece of paper, but recorded through an automated answering system connected to each lawyer's phone; the type you might have at home.

"We should not go in this direction," said one older lawyer. "It's totally insensitive, not what lawyers do, and our clients will hate it because there is no personal interaction." Of course, he didn't realize that it was the clients who were now using voice mail because they didn't have to hire receptionists and other staff to simply take messages on little pink slips. Lawyers are often the last people to understand the implications of new technology.

Or, I could have recalled another meeting at another law firm I was at in the early 1990s where all the lawyers were debating whether to adopt a technology called "electronic mail," or "email," where messages were typed into the computer and sent instantly to other parties over this new thing called the "Internet." Larger documents such as letters or contracts could be "attached" to these emails and when "downloaded," could be modified within the body of the document itself; something one couldn't do with a fax. The partners at the firm decided that one computer in the library would suffice for email; otherwise, they would have to pay for computers on all the lawyers' desks, an Internet connection, and all the security that went along with that. There were flimsy and hollow excuses of why not to use the electronic mail system, and needless to say, that law firm is no longer around.

I could have thought about my own law firm, where the CEO (at the time) was against allowing LinkedIn to be accessible to lawyers from their office computers.

For some reason, I didn't think of these "eureka" or "ah-ha" moments in communications technology, where something new — something we now take for granted today — was introduced to (or withheld from) my coworkers and I.

Instead, I thought of my mother, Diane Wilson, whose sudden and unexpected death in April 2009 was revealed to me not by a sad telephone call, but on Facebook. Death by Facebook, you might say.

I had last seen her right after a long lunch with a close friend I don't see often enough at Pagliacci's in Victoria. After lunch, on the way to the ferry home to Vancouver, I stopped in to see my mother at her apartment, and fixed something on her computer. I vaguely recall her asking me how she could get on Facebook. At the time, I knew little or nothing about Facebook; how things were about to change, for both of us.

Three weeks later, I was at a lacrosse game with my son when my daughter phoned me on my cell. She was at home, totally beside herself, and barely able to string a sentence together. "What's wrong?" I asked. She couldn't tell me because she was in tears. She said I had to leave the lacrosse game and get home right away. She wouldn't say why. I left immediately and drove ten miles home wondering whether she'd been in a car accident, or she'd set the house on fire, or she'd thrown a baseball through our brand new flat screen television.

As soon as I came into the house, she took me by the hand and walked me immediately over to her Facebook page on the iMac, and pointed to the screen. (Remember, I wasn't on Facebook so I wasn't really sure what to look at. At the time, I never expected to be on Facebook, but my daughter and my son were on it constantly.)

My daughter showed me a "status update," posted perhaps 60 minutes previously by my niece in Calgary, which said something like this: "Grandma, we love you, RIP. You're in a better place now."

"What?" I asked myself.

My mom died in her apartment, in her sleep. My brother and my other niece couldn't reach her on the phone for a couple of days. They thought that maybe she was out for a walk, or napping, or out with a friend. My brother and his other daughter drove to my Mom's building in suburban Sidney to check on her. They found she had passed away, and my youngest niece, who lived in Victoria, immediately phoned her sister in Calgary to tell her. My niece in Calgary immediately posted the RIP in her status update on Facebook for the world to see.

When my brother phoned me a few minutes later to give me the sad news in "real time," I already knew what had happened because of his eldest daughter's Facebook post.

I make this point at the very start of the book to emphasize the importance of social networking sites like Facebook, and online communications generally. I also tell this story because of the differing conclusions one could draw from my eldest niece posting my mom's death on Facebook before the rest of the family knew about it.

I've certainly heard the comment more than once, "How could your niece be so insensitive to post your mom's death on Facebook before the rest of the family knew?" In terms of family dynamics, one could say posting my mom's demise on Facebook may not have earned my niece many brownie points for good "online reputation management."

In fairness to her, I don't think my niece was trying to be insensitive. My mom raised my two nieces from the time they were babies, so my mom (their grandmother) was the only mother they had ever really known. Losing her was like losing a "real" mother. My two nieces were in shock and grief, but rather than telephoning her friends (and one would have hoped, her uncle) to share the news and grieve one-on-one, my niece in Calgary did what many people younger than 30 might well have done in the same circumstances. She shared the news with her "online" family, as insensitive as that might appear to her "offline" family.

This struck me as one of those eureka moments where a communication technology I wasn't really familiar with, adopted fully by a particular group (in this case, people younger than 30), landed right in front of me with a big, loud thud. It was Death by Facebook.

1. The Digital Tattoo: Why Maintaining Online Reputations Is Important

The fact that everyone in the world can now be an author, photographer, videographer, and publisher (and I suppose, obituary writer), creates some interesting legal, business, and social issues.

Some of these issues are for businesses, small and large. It's the reason a good half of this book is targeted to business. The following are some questions people in business may want to consider:

- What are people saying about my company, my business, my products, and my brand?

- How can I monitor what people say about my company?

- What should I do if people are saying uncomplimentary or even libelous or slanderous things online about me, my company, and my company's products or services?

- What do I do if someone puts an uncomplimentary video on YouTube about my company or its products?

- What if someone creates a Facebook fan page dedicated to disparaging my brand? Can I sue? Should I sue?

- Are there strategies to adopt to deal with my company's online reputation?

- What if some of the comments that are posted online are from my employees? Can I fire them?

- What if the comments are from my customers?

- If others mention my trademark, can I take legal action?

- If others disclose copyrighted information, how can I stop it?

- If everyone seems to be online these days, should my company have an online presence beyond a mere web page?

- Should we have a Facebook fan page, a regular blog, or other online ways to promote the company, the brand, and the products?

A good portion of this book will attempt to answer these questions, and at least half the book is geared for small-business people who need to understand they're not in Kansas anymore. It is important to know what consumers, employees, and critics are saying about your business so that you can deal with it, either with better public relations or better products. You need to know that you could lose your reputation in the marketplace and all you've worked for in a nanosecond.

This book isn't just a "business book" for companies. Online reputation management also applies to individuals and their activities online. In many ways, online reputation management can be even more important to individuals, whose relationships with family, friends, and coworkers can be detrimentally affected by their online conduct. That conduct may have an affect on them in the job market where momentary lapses of online reason, really bad judgment, and, dare I say stupidity, can be seen by millions of people, especially current and future employers. Online communications, photographs, and videos, potentially read by millions of people, can damage personal reputations, especially the reputation of the person making the comments in the first place.

This might not matter so much to people older than 30. This may be because "older" adults tend to share things with others in more private ways than the Internet, though there are always exceptions. As for those younger than 30, and particularly the 13- to 25-year-old age group that make up the mainstay of Facebook and other social media sites, it's safe to say that there has never been a generation so willing to share its innermost feelings, not to mention outrageous opinions and inappropriate videos and photographs (again, there are always exceptions). The problem is that many of these people don't seem to understand how the comments, photos, and videos posted online can be publicly accessible, profoundly inappropriate, defamatory to others, mind-numbingly stupid, career limiting, and, in some cases, criminal.

From the 15-year-old high school student's perspective, it might be a badge of honor to post photos of the weekend's wayward drunken vodka bender on Facebook, knowing that, as his or her parents aren't "friends" with the student, they won't see what people said about the night in their status updates, or the posted and tagged photographs with all the bottles laying around the house. It might be cool to tell the world he or she belongs to groups that are sexually explicit, or that the person likes to swear like a truck driver on his or her "wall," knowing only his or her "friends" will see it. Or it might be provocative to post (or allow to be posted) digital pictures that are sexually suggestive, or which might belong in *Maxim* magazine or in a Victoria's Secret catalog.

However, it's disingenuous to think one's parents, teachers, or the people close to them (or for that matter, one's future employers), won't one day see the inappropriate photos and comments if the teen or 20-something has 750 friends on Facebook. (How can *anyone* have 750 real friends?)

The reality is that, despite amendments to Facebook's worldwide privacy policies in 2009 and 2010 (thanks, in no small way to the actions of Canada's Privacy Commissioner), it's still possible to see and copy what many users have posted to Facebook. Maybe it's because they haven't figured out Facebook's privacy policies. Despite activating some of those privacy settings, sometimes it's still possible to access Facebook profiles through the "back door," if someone has made comments or posts on public sites. (Who can figure it out? It changes every few months.) Maybe some people don't care as much about privacy as older adults do. Maybe it's like the old VCR machines that always flashed "12:00" because their owners didn't know how to program them. Maybe Facebook's privacy policy is so convoluted and so ever-changing, people give up on it or hope for the best.

The truth is, if comments, photos, or videos are anywhere online, there's a chance they can be (or already have been) accessed and saved by others. The more provocative the content, the more friends the user has as part of his or her network, and the more that person is tagged or makes comments on other sites with his or her Facebook account, the more likely the content will be accessible and recirculated to others, and, I should add, retained in the archives of search engines and data aggregators, or on someone else's computer.

What happens when the 16-year-old who's made outrageous (and perhaps legally defamatory) comments online or has posted (or has allowed to be posted) sexually provocative photos of herself online, or photos of her drunk, is in the job market at 22, expecting to deal with clients of an employer, all of whom might be able to see what she posted (or allowed to be posted) five or six years earlier?

I can only echo what I've been told most of the Deans of Canada's law schools and business schools tell their new students each year. They are warned to watch what they say and do on social media and on their personal blogs or on forums. They are advised to get more professional email addresses than mojokitty69@whatever.com. They're told, in so many words, to "protect their reputations" because, quite frankly, "their reputations matter."

Clean up your Facebook pages. Clean up your blogs. Think before you post or upload. Your prospective employers will be looking for you and at you.

I can tell you firsthand as an employer, we do check online. Almost all employers check the "online footprints" of their potential employees these days. I check my potential employees' online footprint before I go to the trouble of hiring and training them. As an employer, taking stock of my future (or current) employees is easy to do and information is freely available with the click of a mouse.

Employers like me are in, what I hate to call the "real world," and if we can, we'll always check up on our prospective employees because we want to know why we should give the job to them and not someone else. I suppose it's the twenty-first century's version of checking out a reference letter, except we do the checking ourselves, online (or we'll hire an outside company to do it). We'll look for them on Facebook, MySpace, or Twitter, and Google their names. We'll even look for them in Google Images. We'll use Google Alerts. We'll read their blogs. They'll be judged, and indeed employed on the basis of their résumés, their education, their skill sets for the job, their personalities, their work ethics, their communication skills, and how they handled themselves in an interview (as well as on mundane issues such as their salary demands and our ability to pay them). They'll also be judged on the basis of that online footprint in the digital sand they've left for the world to inspect; those pictures of them provocatively dressed that were posted to Facebook or MySpace way back in 2008 that are still public, or the nasty rant about the boss in a 2006 blog post, or the vodka bottles lying around the kitchen at a party in high school where they're tagged on someone else's Facebook page. Conclusions will be drawn. Judgments will be made. Rightly or wrongly, a job candidate's "digital tattoo" may well be part of the hiring equation. It may not be fair, but suck it up; that's how the real world works.

And why not? My competitors are regularly checking the Web to see what I'm doing on it. All my prospective clients do the same thing when they're trying to determine whether to hire me to do their legal work. They'll look for me online everywhere they can. They'll read what's said about me on my firm's website, in media interviews I've done, and in columns I've written for *The Globe and Mail* and the many other publications for which I write.

Although I may use the Internet to check out a future or current employee or client, the consequences of leaving too large a footprint can be very harsh, as discussed in Jeffrey Rosen's article, "The Web Means the End of Forgetting," in *The New York Times* on July 23, 2010:

Examples are proliferating daily: there was the 16-year-old British girl who was fired from her office job for complaining on Facebook, "I'm so totally bored!!"; there was the 66-year-old Canadian psychotherapist who tried to enter the United States but was turned away at the border — and barred permanently from visiting the country — after a border guard's Internet search found that the therapist had written an article in a philosophy journal describing his experiments 30 years ago with LSD.

Rosen also discussed the case of Stacey Snider:

Stacy Snyder, then a 25-year-old teacher in training at Conestoga Valley High School in Lancaster, Pa., posted a photo on her MySpace page that showed her at a party wearing a pirate hat and drinking from a plastic cup, with the caption "Drunken Pirate." After discovering the page, her supervisor at the high school told her the photo was unprofessional, and the Dean of Millersville University School of Education, where Snyder was enrolled, said she was promoting drinking in virtual view of her underage students. As a result, days before Snyder's scheduled graduation, the university denied her a teaching degree. Snyder sued, arguing that the university had violated her First Amendment rights by penalizing her for her (perfectly legal) after-hours behavior. But in 2008, a federal district judge rejected the claim, saying that because Snyder was a public employee whose photo didn't relate to matters of public concern, her "Drunken Pirate" post was not protected speech.

He goes on to say:

All around the world, political leaders, scholars, and citizens are searching for responses to the challenge of preserving control of our identities in a digital world that never forgets ... Alex Türk, the French data-protection commissioner, has called for a "constitutional right to oblivion" that would allow citizens to maintain a greater degree of anonymity online and in public places ... the European Union helped finance a campaign called "Think B4 U post!" that urges young people to consider the "potential consequences" of publishing photos of themselves or their friends without "thinking carefully" and asking permission.

After reading this, if you haven't run back to your computer to adjust your privacy settings, delete some photographs, and get others de-tagged, just remember Web 2.0 isn't as private as you might think, and even if you do adjust your privacy settings today so future employers can't see anything, there's still a chance something embarrassing, provocative, or career limiting is available on someone else's computer where the privacy settings haven't been tightened, or it's still archived in Google or another website that collects, retains, aggregates, and stores data.

Think of everything you say and do online, whether on Facebook, Twitter, personal blogs, forums, YouTube, or on other social media sites as your own, personal "digital tattoo." We all know how hard and painful it is to get tattoos removed, don't we? And if we don't, we will.

2. Who Is This Book For?

This book is divided between reputation management for individuals and reputation management for businesses. Whether you're a business person looking for advice on protecting a brand's reputation or your company's reputation, or you're a parent or schoolteacher wanting to know more about protecting individual reputations, I can tell you this book is *not* for experts in web analytics, marketing theory, branding behavior, search engine optimization, online survey strategy, or for that matter, child psychologists studying the strange animal called the teenage brain. There are other books out there that will help you deal with those issues in more thorough, academic, and detailed ways if that's what you want. This book is introductory in nature, written to give you a general understanding of online reputation management issues.

Although this book is meant to be educational, it's not an academic textbook or a PhD thesis either. I like to stay around the 5,000-foot level, so that readers aren't burdened with too many details, yet they can come away with a good, basic understanding of what online reputation management is, why it's important, and what happens when things go horribly wrong. I do that by relating stories; "war stories" if you like. That's because people can relate to stories and learn from them.

I also discuss in general ways, without getting mired in technical detail, what tools you can use to manage your online reputation so that you, your company, your child, or your student isn't on the front page of the newspaper because something he or she did is now posted on Facebook, YouTube, or Twitter. Parents, teachers, and school counselors might find this book to be useful, not only for themselves, but for the children they raise and the ones they teach.

It's written in such a way that you might actually finish reading it in a night or two, and be ready to read other books on the topic. Chapters are broken into distinct topic areas that you can read without necessarily having to have read other chapters beforehand. For example, if you're a parent, teacher, or school counselor, you might *not* be interested in corporate branding issues, copyright, or trademark law, or what you should consider when drafting employee social media policies. Those chapters are targeted at people in business.

However, you might be interested in how to find the metadata in Word documents your students have emailed to you (so you can see if the essay has been written by someone else), or you might be very interested in Chapter 7 on sexting, cyberbullying, and online academic cheating, and the excellent research into those areas being undertaken by Pew Internet & American Life Project (a US-based think tank studying issues on the attitudes and trends shaping modern life in the United States and the world), and the Cyberbullying Research Center (CRC).

Parents, teachers and business people might be interested in Chapter 5, which deals with the importance of apologies when you've made a mistake that affects your brand or reputation, and the tools you can use to craft a better apology than no apology at all, (or one that has obviously been written for public relations or legal reasons). Good apologies can save reputations. Bad ones can ruin them.

Or you might just want to see the various online tools which I discuss in Chapter 9. This chapter will help you discover ways of finding out what is being said about you, your business, or your products online.

Chapter 11 includes interesting news, facts, and information that is illustrative of issues in online reputation management.

One big problem is that things change quickly. By way of example, Facebook's privacy policy changed at least two times since October 2009 when I first started working on this book, and legal decisions from courts around the world continue to affect and change the online landscape regularly. By the time you read this book, some of the factual information may have changed. The practical advice I give you — the dos, don'ts, and other lessons about online reputation management as well as the sources where you can get further information — won't change, so I assure you, this book is worth reading.

Finally, this is also not a law book. The law regarding reputation management is interdisciplinary, complex, full of nuances, and always changing. I try to cover the basic legal concepts in this area broadly, without getting mired in details or legal niceties, and even then, the legal discussion is general in nature. You should not presume that the legal issues that I discuss are meant to supplant or replace the advice of legal professionals who would review the law as it applies to your particular circumstances, or within your particular jurisdiction. If you think something you have posted or otherwise published might be defamatory or might injure another's reputation, or if you think your own good reputation has been damaged by the comments of someone in an email, a blog post, a message board, a forum, on Twitter, on Facebook, on YouTube, or something as mundane as in a newspaper, you should be talking to a lawyer who knows something about this area. If you don't know where to find one, email me at twilson@boughton.ca or tonywilson1@gmail.com and I'll try to point you in the right direction. Or just Google me. I have a fairly large digital footprint, but I always make sure everything (I'll repeat — everything) that's said by me or is written about me online is there because I want it there. That's the first lesson, I suppose, in good reputation management. Take control of it. It's yours.

In any event, I hope the book will, at the very least, instill a sense of urgency to *monitor* and *manage*, and perhaps even *sculpt* what is said about you, and indeed, what is said by you, online so that you can protect yourself not only from others, but from yourself too.

1
AN OVERVIEW OF SOCIAL MEDIA

Like the telephone in the early twentieth century; the fax machine in the '70s; voice mail in the '80s; email and online forums in the '90s; and blogs, instant messaging, and text messaging on smartphones in the '00s; in this decade, online communication through social networking and other social media is the way many people relate to each other now.

The online environment we live in today, when compared with the environment in 1990 or even 2000, is quite unlike any in which we have ever lived. It's a different world than the one I grew up in. This world has its own customs, protocols, conventions, inside jokes, and taboos.

The Internet wasn't invented by former US Vice President Al Gore. It really started in 1969 as a US Department of Defense project called Advanced Research Projects Agency Network (ARPANET) and connected four US universities to exchange information across a network of computers. The web browser only came into existence with the development of Mosaic in 1993. In the mid-'90s, commercial services such as AOL and CompuServe started offering access to the Internet through subscribed services.

A survey done in December 2009, performed by Pew Internet & American Life Project, revealed that —

- 74 percent of all American adults (ages 18 and older) use the Internet;

- 60 percent of American adults use broadband connections at home; and

- 55 percent of American adults connect to the Internet wirelessly, either through a WiFi or related connection on their laptop, BlackBerry, iPhone, or other wireless device.

As for email, The Radicati Group, a technology market research company headquartered in Palo Alto, California, estimates that 247 billion emails per day were sent in 2009 (of which 81 percent were estimated to be spam, leaving perhaps 47 billion legitimate emails per day). The Radicati Group also estimated that the average corporate user sends and receives approximately 110 messages daily, and around 18 percent of those emails are spam, which includes actual spam and what is termed graymail (i.e., unwanted newsletters, alerts). As of May 2010, there were 2.9 billion email user accounts, and this is expected to grow to 3.8 billion by 2014.

In The Radicati Group's "Email Statistics Report, 2010" (available at Radicati.com), in 2010, 75 percent of all email accounts were owned by consumers, and 25 percent were owned by businesses. This 75/25 ratio is expected to stay constant until 2014. Of all the email users, 47 percent are located in Asia and the Pacific (i.e., China, India, Japan, Oceania), while 23 percent of email accounts are in Europe, and 14 percent in North America.

1. Networking Sites

In July 2010, Facebook reported that it had more than 500 million registered users; if it were a country, it would be the third largest nation in the world after China and India. (By 2015, it may surpass both!) Facebook states that the average user has 130 friends, and that people spend more than 700 billion minutes per month on Facebook. Its users share more than 30 billion pieces of content each month. The average user is connected to 80 pages, groups, and events, and creates 90 pieces of content monthly. Fifty percent of Facebook's active users log on every day. Interestingly enough, only 30 percent of Facebook's users are in the United States. There are more than 150 million active users currently accessing Facebook through mobile devices such as BlackBerrys, iPhones, and other mobile telephones.

Facebook's own statistics show that people who use Facebook on their mobile devices are twice as active on Facebook as laptop or desktop users. You wonder why television is dying? Everyone's eyes seem to be on their computers accessing Facebook and other social networking sites.

Whereas Facebook is for friends connecting with other friends, LinkedIn is for businesspeople connecting with other businesspeople, whether for jobs, business opportunities, profile upgrading, or other networking where one knows that other businesspeople will be looking. It had 75 million registered users in 2010.

Facebook and LinkedIn aren't the only social networking sites that people belong to and use. What social networking site you use depends on where you are in the world, and what you're looking for in a social networking site (i.e., business, pleasure, music, dating, shopping), your age, your occupation, your first language, the "market niche" of the site, and what network your other friends and contacts are using. There's Bebo, MySpace, Friendster, hi5, orkut, PerfSpot, Yahoo! 360°, Zorpia, Netlog, Sales Spider, StumbleUpon, Delicious, Digg, Classmates, Xanga and many more (especially if you include all the dating sites). In fact, Apple launched Ping, a music social networking site the day I wrote this paragraph. However, in this book, I'm going to concentrate on Facebook because it seems to be the one site where everyone "is" and where everyone makes the most mistakes. At least until something else comes along to replace it.

2. Video Sharing

YouTube, the online video-sharing platform, announced in 2010 that 2 billion YouTube videos were viewed per day. In 2010, it celebrated five years of existence. The company was created by three employees of PayPal: Steve Chen, Chad Hurley, and Jawed Karim. They developed what would become the world's leading video-sharing platform. YouTube has made it possible for anyone with a video camera (or a camera, or a cell phone that can shoot video), to post a video on the Internet that can be seen by hundreds of millions of people almost immediately.

YouTube is not without criticism. It relies on its users to highlight videos or content that can be arguably pornographic, that contains copyrighted or trademarked property owned by others, or otherwise contains questionable content that might be deemed defamatory or a breach of YouTube's terms of service that all who upload must agree to.

Clean Cut Media, a website studying the influences of media and pop culture, states that YouTube is the fourth largest destination on the Internet, and the largest video-sharing site. It has 300 million worldwide visitors per month allowing in excess of 5 billion video streams per month. Every day, close to 3.5 million people visit YouTube. The number of videos posted on YouTube in 2008 was estimated to be 83.4 million, and some sources believe the number to be closer to 150 million in 2010.

The market research company, comScore, states the obvious when it claims that YouTube is the "dominant provider of online video" in the United States. More than 14 billion videos were viewed in May 2010, and 24 hours of new videos are uploaded to YouTube every minute.

YouTube has created its own celebrity culture whereby so-called "ordinary people" become famous for no other reason than having appeared on YouTube. Or, because they shot a YouTube video that becomes popular and goes viral. For example, Chad Vader: Day Shift Manager, Amber Lee Ettinger also known as Obama Girl, Chris Crocker for his sobbing rant: "Leave Britney Alone," and "Bree" for LonelyGirl15 (a fictional story of teenage girl and the video diary of her life).

YouTube also has an interesting business model, at least for the "pirated" clips you can see on YouTube if you look for them. Pirated clips of movies, TV shows, and other copyrighted productions posted by third parties that you'd think would be pulled off of YouTube by the legal departments of Paramount, 20th Century Fox, or other copyright owners, are often allowed to remain on YouTube as long as YouTube and the copyright holder split the ad revenue generated from the page the clips are on!

Business, nonprofits, "traditional" media, politicians, and interest groups of all types have taken advantage of YouTube's ability to get video messages to individuals without paying for distribution; in a way, democratizing the "airwaves" in a way television cannot.

Whether you like it or not, YouPorn (the pornographic website modeled on YouTube but which is in no way related to YouTube), is the largest free pornographic site in the world and has been ranked among the top 50 most accessed websites in the world.

3. Cell Phones and Texting

The very first mobile telephones were put into New York City police cars in 1924, although cell phones or mobile phones didn't become prevalent until the early 1990s (when some of them looked like, and were as heavy as, bricks). The adoption of this technology has been astounding and transformative, especially in the developing world; in some areas in Asia and Africa, the finance and development of land lines has taken a backseat to the adoption of mobile telephone infrastructure.

By the end of 2009, there were an estimated 4.6 billion mobile phones in use throughout the world. China has a staggering 786,000,000 mobile phone subscribers. India has more than 600,000,000 mobile phone subscribers and the United States has more than 285,000,000. Even less developed countries such as Pakistan (97,000,000 subscribers) and Nigeria (64,000,000 subscribers) have large and growing mobile phone markets.

Most cell phones manufactured since 2005 have the ability to use Short Message Service (SMS) or text message if the subscriber pays for it. Although anyone older than 50 might find the idea of texting with one's cell phone ridiculous when one could just as easily phone the person directly, texting short messages is often used when it's inconvenient or impractical to have a telephone conversation, such as during a meeting, when the surrounding noise (or company) makes a telephone conversation problematic, or if you're a student, while in class. If you're a parent and your kids don't pick up their cell phones or check their voice mail, rest assured the kids will certainly check their text messages. Remember, you're more likely to reach them with a text these days than a phone call.

Of all mobile or cell phones, 75 percent have text capabilities. SMS text messaging, where the sender is limited to 140 (or 160) characters, may well be the most utilized text data application in the world today, even more prevalent than email given its widespread usage in China, India, and other parts of Asia. In China, it's estimated that 700 billion text messages were sent in 2007. In the Philippines, more than 400 million text messages a day are sent (142 billion text messages a year). Text messaging is so prevalent in India, that service providers text transit alerts, cricket scores, and allow for mobile billing and banking services to be performed via text messaging. Over the years, text messaging has expanded to include digital images, sounds, and video sent via Multimedia Messaging Service (MMS).

There have been unfortunate social side effects of the use of texting on mobile phones. Driving while texting is one obvious example and many jurisdictions have banned all use of mobile devices while driving given that automobile accidents are more likely to happen when the driver is texting a message and not watching the road (duh). Another is the misuse of language that has evolved through the use of texting shorthand (e.g., lol, 2day, lmao, b4, gr8); changing English and other languages (e.g., in China, the numbers 520 sound like the Mandarin words for "I love you").

Perhaps the worst social side effect from texting, and one that relates to reputation management, involves "sexting," where teenagers try to impress (or entice) each other by sending either sexual content within a text message, or sexual images they have taken of themselves with their cell phones. What's worse is when these private communications are re-sent to others; the sender (often being a teenage boy who received the "sext") is potentially in possession of child pornography and subject to criminal prosecution. If re-texted to others, these sexts could well lead to convictions for distribution of child pornography. (Sexting is discussed in greater detail in Chapter 7.)

We can't forget golfer Tiger Woods' exploits (discussed in Chapter 3), that were exposed after his wife Elin found sexually charged text messages on Tiger's cell phone. A few of Tiger's girlfriends actually kept these text messages, eventually publishing them on websites and releasing them to the media. (Texts aren't private, Tiger!)

4. Twitter

According to Twitter's website: "Twitter is a real-time information network powered by people all around the world that lets you share and discover what's happening now." Twitter enables users to send and read other users' messages (called "tweets"), which are text-based posts of no more than 140 characters to a mass audience of "followers." Tweets are visible publicly, as is the very intention of Twitter. Users may subscribe to other authors' tweets.

San Antonio-based market research firm Pear Analytics analyzed 2,000 tweets which were sent in English from the United States over a two-week period in August 2009 and categorized the tweets as the following:

- Pointless babble (what one might also call "small talk"): 40.55 percent
- Conversational: 37.55 percent
- Pass-along value: 8.7 percent
- Self-promotion: 5.85 percent
- Spam: 3.75 percent
- News: 3.6 percent

There were more than 100 million registered Twitter users as of May, 2010. The US Library of Congress stated that it will be acquiring, and permanently storing the entire archive of public Twitter posts since 2006.

5. Social Media Is Here to Stay

Digital communications are here to stay, and communication through social media will only get more prevalent until something else supplants it. Online forums, blogs, and social networking sites such as Facebook have revolutionized the way people communicate with each other and share their day-to-day experiences, their opinions (thoughtful, bad, ridiculous, poorly informed, or just plain dull), their photographs, and their videos. It's never been so easy to "publish" something, and have it read by dozens, hundreds, or even millions of people, almost instantaneously. It could be about a particular product or service offered by a business, a meal at a restaurant, the quality of rooms in a hotel, or a high school teacher or university professor. It could be about a particular person. And yes, you can read a death announcement before anyone else in the family hears about it.

A survey released by Pew Internet & American Life Project on July 2, 2010, posed a question (which was framed as two questions in the positive and the negative) that respondents were asked whether they agreed or disagreed:

"In 2020, when I look at the big picture and consider my personal friendships, marriage, and other relationships, I see that the Internet has mostly been a *positive/negative* force on my social world. And this will only grow more true in the future."

Eighty-five percent of respondents agreed with the positive statement and 14 percent agreed with the negative statement.

Said the Pew Internet report: "Humans'" use of the Internet's capabilities for communication for creating, cultivating, and continuing social relationships is undeniable. Many enthusiastically cited their personal experiences as examples and several noted that they had met their spouses through "Internet-borne interaction."

Many of the respondents agreed that "time spent online robs time from important face-to-face relationships; the Internet fosters mostly shallow relationships; [using] the Internet to engage in social connection exposes private information; the Internet allows people to silo themselves, limiting their exposure to new ideas; and the Internet is being used to engender intolerance."

Respondents also noted that "geography is no longer an obstacle to making and maintaining connections." However, others observed that there will be "variations of depression caused by the lack of meaningful quality relationships."

There may also be new ways of how users define friendship and privacy that are different than how we might define those concepts or use those words in the future.

Some of the respondents commented on how they met their spouse online, reconnected with old school friends, and stayed in touch with family and friends overseas. These will all be normal things for those born of the Internet age.

So let's look now at why it is important to manage your online reputation, and some strategies to do it.

2
MANAGING YOUR REPUTATION

Being a regular reader of *The New Yorker*, I recall a cartoon by Barbara Smaller in 1999, where two preschool children were talking in front of a locker about what they wanted to be when they grew up. One said to the other, quite prophetically, "Actually, I'm hoping what I'm going to be when I grow up hasn't been invented yet."

Online reputation management falls right into that category. In 2000, you might have known that emails could be forwarded everywhere and to anyone, so you should be careful what you said in an email. Once you hit the send button, you can never get it back, and whatever you said, good or bad, could be read (and re-sent) by millions.

In 2005, before Facebook, LinkedIn, Twitter, YouTube, smartphones, flash mobs, and rampant SMS texting, trying to tell someone that what he or she posted online could damage his or her "reputation" might have sounded prudish, like one's mother, warning her daughter of the perils of low-cut dresses, too much makeup, or tight jeans.

Online reputation management is an area of law and public relations that, although "invented," is still in its infancy. It straddles a number of legal and nonlegal disciplines:

1. It involves the communications that people have online and this involves computer and Internet law. Emails, text messages,

digital photographs, and videos from cell phones can be sent instantaneously to anyone in the world; even newspapers eager to expose the story of an Olympic gold medalist smoking marijuana from a bong at a party!

2. Online reputation management involves the laws of slander, libel, and defamation on the one hand, and freedom of speech on the other. Can you exercise your right to free speech online, or must you be concerned whether the comments made over the Internet can be freely made without regard to the legal rules of slander, libel, and defamation? If you yell fire in a crowded movie theater and there is no fire, or you defame someone in the newspaper, serious legal consequences will follow. But what about the things you say online?

3. It involves the "rules" (more accurately, the legal terms and conditions enforceable by judges in courts under the law of contract), that websites, Internet service providers, and social networking sites such as Facebook, LinkedIn, and YouTube require you to contractually agree to before you can participate in any online activity. In order to participate, you must agree to their terms of use, and this binds you to those contractual provisions, including the ownership of the photographs and other material you post. That's why you always have to "click here" if you agree. This is your contractual signature.

4. It involves intellectual property law such as trademark law, in respect of the use of someone's brand. If images, videos, or artistic or written works are circulated digitally, it involves copyright law and who owns the rights to those works.

5. It involves the law of privacy and what sort of personal information can and can't be collected by businesses and other organizations about individuals. Related to this are the obligations that social networking sites such as Facebook have to keep certain personal information private.

6. It involves the management of our personal and corporate "reputations"; our "brands" if you will, and what others think of us.

Certainly large corporations such as Apple, Disney, Procter & Gamble, Starbucks, Microsoft, United Airlines, Exxon, and BP have brands and reputations to protect (and as we shall see, to damage as well).

Noncommercial entities also have brands and reputations to protect and foster, even though they're not trying to sell you anything. Greenpeace, Médecins Sans Frontières, the United Nations, FBI, and RCMP are examples of organizations that should be just as conscious and vigilant as private companies in the protection of their brands and reputations, if not more so. Unfortunately, at least one of these organizations has had an online reputation disaster, which will be discussed in Chapter 3.

Celebrities and public figures such as Tiger Woods, Michael Phelps, David Letterman, Martha Stewart, Paris Hilton, Lady Gaga, Conrad Black, Senator John Edwards, and Sarah the Duchess of York, have brands and reputations to protect and cultivate. For some of them, their name is their brand, and lucrative endorsement contracts by cereal, automobile, watch, and athletic companies will be at risk if the person making the endorsement has a problem with his or her own reputation. The spokesperson's damaged reputation could damage the brand and reputation of the product. However, a questionable reputation may simply add to the brand's appeal in certain unique market segments where a bad-boy or bad-girl panache is actually cultivated. (Do Paris Hilton and Pamela Anderson really care about those sex tapes? Have the tapes damaged or "enhanced" their reputations?)

We all have reputations and our own personal brands that can get damaged, perhaps irreparably, from our online conduct or from our conduct that is captured and distributed online. Just ask two Winnipeg, Manitoba teachers who were filmed on a cell phone at a pep rally performing mock sex acts. They were fired; leaving their careers in tatters. Reputation matters, even if we're not celebrities. In this century, what happens in Vegas doesn't stay in Vegas anymore. It can be on the Internet in seconds and seen by millions in a matter of days. It's the era of the digital tattoo.

At the corporate or business level, brand management is a multibillion-dollar industry. Although some would say the overriding objective of branding and the management of corporate brands is to get consumers to purchase the products manufactured or distributed by those companies and drive up sales, part of brand management is also dealing with the crises that threaten the brand every so often. Something that comes to mind: the famous Tylenol murders of 1982 where someone laced capsules of Tylenol with potassium cyanide in the United States, leading to a worldwide recall of all Tylenol products and crisis management of epic proportions.

There have been similar branding crises, or you might say, "public relations crises" in Canada. Maple Leaf Foods had a serious outbreak of a disease called listeriosis in its meatpacking plant near Toronto in 2008. Consumers ate deli meat that was infected with the bacteria and became sick. At least 20 people died of the disease.

At the time of writing this book, Toyota's brand was suffering badly due to an alleged faulty gas pedal that supposedly wouldn't allow drivers to decelerate.

Also at the time of writing this book, millions of gallons of crude oil was spewing from a deep sea underwater well operated by BP, which BP did a disastrous job of containing (and perhaps an equally bad job of managing its reputation in the process).

Who could ignore the plight of "living brands" such as Martha Stewart, jailed for securities offenses; or Conrad Black, in jail for obstruction of justice; Senator John Edwards for having his assistant be the fall guy for his love child with another aide; or Tiger Woods, whose fondness for waitresses, hostesses, and at least one porn star resulted in the cancellation of numerous lucrative endorsement contracts. His name continues to give fodder to the tabloid newspapers and late-night TV monologues.

These are certainly brand crises, but as we'll see, they aren't so much *online* brand crises, or at least, crises directly caused by online activities. Online brand crises happen when a dissatisfied customer posts a song on YouTube about an airline breaking his guitar and the video gets millions of hits in a matter of weeks. Or when employees of a pizza restaurant film themselves doing disgusting things with the food they're making and upload it to YouTube for millions of customers to see. Or when officers of a police force respected around the world repeatedly fire a Taser at a tired, confused, and unarmed Polish immigrant at an airport, and he dies; the entire event being captured on a video camera and eventually posted to YouTube.

A corporate reputation built up over decades can be tarnished by one disgruntled customer who posts a bad review about your business online to a site like TripAdvisor or an exposé to YouTube, or by a status update on Facebook that berates your business. Or if someone creates a Facebook page dedicated to how bad the page's authors (who may in fact be employees of the manufacturer or distributer) think your product or service is. Or if someone tweets to thousands of followers (which can be re-tweeted to hundreds of thousands more) about a problem with a product or a service provided by a business like yours. Result? Immediate, instantaneous, and damaging consumer-led revolts.

Individuals like you and I have reputations to protect. We have to think of our personal reputations as "brands" as well. It's not only Tiger Woods' and the Duchess of York's reputations that are at stake because they're famous. Our own reputations are at stake by the things said about us online and especially by the things said *by* us online.

We all have brands and reputations to protect, don't we? Even if we work in a bank, a law office, or if we're students or teachers in a high school. Again, think of it like a tattoo; interesting and provocative when you have it done when you're young, but painful and very expensive to remove when you get older — if you can remove it at all.

Our reputations can be harmed by the people around us, people in our online community, and more often than not, by ourselves. In that sense, we have to protect ourselves from others, but we also have to protect ourselves from ourselves.

3
WHY REPUTATION MANAGEMENT IS IMPORTANT

Teenage girls aren't the only ones whose mothers have warned them for generations about their reputations. In the online context, it probably means a teenage girl's reputation for her relations (or, more accurately, her perceived relations) with boys.

Consumers almost always use reputation as a tool to aid in their decision making. How does a person know that lawyer A is "better" than lawyer B? Or that Dr. S is a better dentist than Dr. Y? How does a consumer of those services decide whether the dentist or lawyer he or she wants to use is the best for the task at hand?

How do you choose the right neighborhood to buy your first house, or choose a school near that house for your young family to go to, or the college or university for your kids once they leave high school? How do you know what hotel to stay at in Cairo or Istanbul, and whether the hotels you found on the Internet are good? How do you know whether the company you're looking at for a bicycle tour of the Dordogne will be honest?

Price may be a factor in all of these decisions. Dentist A may be too expensive. Lawyer B's hourly rate is too high for something simple. You may decide you don't need a five-star hotel in Cairo (trust me, you do). The bike tour company in the Dordogne caters to the über-rich.

Lawyers are taught from the first day they enter law school that their professional reputation is all they have to offer and they carry it with them wherever they go in their career. This may well be said of other professions and callings as well. As a lawyer myself, I know that some of my colleagues have reputations for being very aggressive lawyers, "pit bulls" you could say, taking no prisoners in any legal dispute and being fierce and unrelenting in the courtroom; feared or loathed by their opponents on the other side.

Knowing that litigation can cost a client as much as the disputed claim and cause all sorts of misery (you could lose the case, after all, and still have to pay both your and the other side's legal bills), a different lawyer might have the reputation of being a "problem solver," "a reasonable person to deal with on the other side" that is professional in all respects, while still protecting his or her client's interests. These lawyers are not pit bulls because that's not their style. Their "value" is their common sense and their ability to persuade and bring people to a settlement or a deal.

A lawyer might also have a reputation as an expert in particular areas of law, and sometimes, this reputation is bestowed by his or her peers by ranking organizations who send questionnaires to other lawyers at the bar in the same field, to assess their anonymous opinions concerning the lawyer being inquired about. Organizations such as Martindale-Hubbell, Lexpert, and Who's Who Legal do this regularly.

A reputation for being a pit bull and not being particularly liked by one's colleagues might be the best recommendation for a lawyer who fashions his or her reputation in that light. "I'm a pit bull. I know I am. The people that hire me, hire me because I'm a pit bull. That's my reputation, and it works for me." (They used to call them hired guns in the old west!)

A lawyer's reputation may also be less than stellar. The lawyer took on a case in an area of law that he or she didn't know enough about. The lawyer didn't know the right case law. The lawyer charged too much for the work that was done. The lawyer didn't finish it on time. The lawyer missed a deadline. The lawyer missed an appointment and didn't return calls promptly. The lawyer is being sued by other clients. The lawyer is uninspiring in court. The lawyer doesn't exude confidence. The lawyer is being reviewed or disciplined by his or her law society. The lawyer's name is in the paper for drunk driving or some other offense.

Let's look at a practical example of a lawyer's reputation, just to illustrate the point. A lawyer colleague of mine called me in a panic recently because one of his big clients had asked for a "second opinion" on a major piece of Intellectual Property litigation. I've seen his work, and it's good. However, he's at a small firm without a big brand name. The client sought the second opinion from another lawyer who I knew also to be quite competent in her area. But she's at a brand name law firm back east.

The lawyer at the big firm has a reputation for "poaching" or at least, trying to poach other lawyers' clients when she can. That is, she tries to maneuver clients away from their current lawyers to her. She'll lunch with or promote a client she knows has been well served for years by another firm, and when asked to give a second opinion about one of her competitors (and his or her legal work), it will always be critical, or if there's praise, it'll be faint. Now maybe this is fine in banking and other commercial services where everyone understands that "it's war out there" and, of course, clients are always free to do what they want and go where they will. However, the lawyers I call my colleagues would never actively poach another lawyer's client away. It's certainly not my style. I rely too much on referrals from other lawyers to get a reputation for poaching their clients. I wouldn't get referrals from them if they knew I was always after their clients.

The lawyer at the big firm I mentioned above? She didn't care that other lawyers talked about her over drinks and in private conversations as "a good lawyer, but she poaches clients." This was why some lawyers would not, on principle, send any referrals to her. Ever. If they're asked to give a recommendation, the praise will be businesslike, brief, and faint.

I use the example of a lawyer's reputation from one end of the spectrum to the other (good reputation to bad), to make the point that reputation isn't so much what *you* think of *yourself*, but what *others* think of *you*. If you're the person whose reputation is being evaluated, what others think of you may well have emanated from your own character and behavior. A reputation for gruffness, aggression, a take-no-prisoners pit bull approach in a lawyer, may be just what a client needs in the courtroom to win. That reputation will get around. On the other end of the spectrum, a lawyer's behavior in terms of not returning phone calls, not making deadlines, not being "up on the law," or not being very good will also get around. If you poach someone's client, or engage in activities that might not be acceptable in your business, that too will get around — especially over "cocktail chatter" when you're not around to hear the gossip.

Similar questions could be asked, with the necessary changes, about a dentist, or a doctor, or a contractor you want to hire to do renovations on your house, a realtor you want to engage to sell your house, or a teacher at your child's school, or a host of other people you want to engage to help you do something.

If you're in business, it applies equally to the partners you take on in that business, the bankers you use, the suppliers you deal with, and the advertising and marketing company you want to engage. I suppose, most importantly, it applies to the employees you want to hire.

1. Damaged Reputations

To understand how important reputation is, I think we should look at some examples of reputations that have been damaged.

1.1 A Tiger by the tail

I suppose I could just say the name Tiger Woods, and make this a very short chapter, because most people in the world were aware of his stellar family man image, the beautiful Swedish wife, the two children, the dog, and his reputation for being the best and the wealthiest golfer on the planet, not to mention the kind of guy you'd like to have as your neighbor. However, it is one of the best examples of what can go wrong when a person's reputation is damaged, particularly if that damage is self-inflicted.

Woods' unprecedented success in golf lead to lucrative endorsement contracts from Nike, TAG Heuer, Titleist, General Mills, American Express, Accenture, Gillette, Gatorade, and many others over the years. *Golf Digest* reported that he had earned almost $770 million between 1996 and 2007, some of the earnings were from golf, but most of this money came from his very lucrative endorsement contracts. As for golf, remember, Woods won the Masters in 1997, 2001, 2002, and 2005; the US Open in 2000, 2002, and 2008, and the PGA Championship in 1999, 2000, 2006, and 2007. This doesn't include the international tournaments he won.

Corporations with products and services to sell love winners, because winners help them sell cars, watches, breakfast cereal, energy drinks, financial services, sports equipment, and a wide range of other products and services. It's part of the madness of crowds, and worshipping the living gods that walk among us. It's crazy, but it's the reality we live in. If you don't like it, I know a monastery in Italy you can move into to get away from it all!

Woods had the world by the tail in 2009. A stellar reputation as the best golfer in the world; the good looking boy next door worth almost $1 billion at 35 years of age — wealthy beyond words. This struck many as a testament to the American Dream; a dream still available to anyone who worked hard and excelled at what they did.

That all came crashing down at the end of 2009, when it was reported Woods had left his driveway at two in the morning in his vehicle, and collided with a hedge, a fire hydrant, a tree, and possibly a nine iron — not necessarily in that order. He was treated for facial lacerations after the accident, but declined to comment on it. There were early reports of his wife, Elin Nordegren, rescuing him from the car by using a nine iron to break the window and heroically pulling him out of the vehicle. Of course, that seemed a bit strange given the photographs of the front fender of the SUV that appeared in magazines and newspapers all over the world.

The silence from Woods' camp didn't help dispel rumors of marital problems between the two spouses that were disclosed in the *National Enquirer* a day before Woods' escapade in the Escalade. The *National Enquirer* had reported that Woods was having an affair with a nightclub hostess named Rachel Uchitel, which was denied at the time by the hostess.

We've all suspected by now that Nordegren wasn't trying to rescue her husband by using the nine iron to free him from a burning car. Rather, Woods' public relations department was working overtime to ensure that its client's reputation and that of his wife, met the expectations of his adoring fans, his admiring public, and his soon to be very concerned corporate sponsors. Woods' crisis management team went into overdrive.

Days after the spin doctors said Woods had been rescued from the SUV, a waitress in San Diego with the name of Jaimee Grubbs told *US Weekly* about her two-year affair with Woods, which was supported by numerous text messages from Woods that substantiated her story.

Following Grubbs, ten other women, including at least one porn star, and several waitresses or hostesses claimed to have affairs, trysts, or casual sexual encounters with Woods. The whole affair became surreal when Uchitel flew to Los Angeles from New York to meet with her celebrity lawyer Gloria Allred. Although Uchitel denied the affair with Woods, her lawyer told the media she would hold a press conference about the relationship with Woods the next day, but hours before the scheduled press conference was to happen, it was abruptly canceled, leading to speculation that this public press conference about a very private matter was a ploy to extract hush money from Woods for her silence.

Over the weeks, stories circulated about multiple partners, prostitutes, threesomes, and payments made by Woods to keep his other partners quiet. As far as my earlier comment that Woods was the kind of guy you'd love to have as your neighbor, he was reported in the *New York Daily News* to have slept with 121 women, including his next-door neighbor's 21-year-old daughter whom he'd first met when she was 14. Oops! What was it I said about Woods being the sort of guy you'd want as your next door neighbor?

It was a public relations disaster for Woods, and a nightmare for his wife and his family. But it was also a PR catastrophe for his sponsors and for the golfing fraternity in general, having hitched their star to Woods' wagon. However, if you were in the PR or crisis-management business, or you worked for a media outlet that reported on celebrities, December 2009 must have been manna from heaven. Especially when some of Woods' sexual partners (including porn star Joslyn James) started releasing the graphic sexual text messages between Woods and her.

Woods, and his good guy-next-door image, was shattered in the space of two weeks. Some sponsors terminated or suspended their relationship with him quickly. Gillette stopped their company's ad campaign featuring Woods.

Accenture, AT&T, and General Motors canceled their endorsement contracts with him. Others de-emphasized him in their advertising in various markets in the world. Accenture said in a statement:

"For the past six years, Accenture and Tiger Woods have had a very successful sponsorship arrangement and his achievements on the golf course have been a powerful metaphor for business success in

Accenture's advertising. However, given the circumstances of the last two weeks, after careful consideration and analysis, the company has determined that he is no longer the right representative for its advertising."

Accenture concluded by saying it "wishes only the best for Tiger Woods and his family."

Economists at the University of California suggested that shareholders of companies who had endorsement relationships with Woods may have lost between $5 billion and $12 billion.

Woods attempted to salvage his reputation by characterizing his deeds as part of an "illness" and enrolling himself in a treatment facility for sex addiction, although many people saw this as public relations management more than anything else. Bad behavior seems less bad or more explainable if it is somehow caused by an illness or addiction. If Woods simply wanted to have sex with 121 women because he could, this would be bad behavior, but if there was something medically wrong that could be packaged as an illness that could be treated by counseling and therapy, maybe it's not so bad after all. He's not a bad guy at all. He's a patient and he has an illness. He can recover if he is treated. He can be redeemed.

Whether Woods' PR department or his sponsors demanded that he seek treatment, and whether the celebrity treatment industry exists purely for PR purposes, seek treatment he did, and he's returned to golfing. Of course, his wife has divorced him, receiving an estimated $750 million settlement in the process.

1.2 Other damaging scandals

As tarnished as the following reputations became, they weren't online reputations, or should I say, the damage done wasn't started because of something that was done by them or about them online. The situations were sent around the world online by news media, blogs, and YouTube after their dubious actions had taken place.

Bernard Madoff was a stockbroker, investment advisor, and former Chairman of NASDAQ, whose clients included Fortis Investments; Citigroup; Deutsche Bank; CNN television host, Larry King; actors John Malkovich and Kevin Bacon; trusts belonging to Henry Kissinger; Steven Spielberg; Jeffrey Katzenberg; and a number of foundations, charities, and universities had billions invested with him.

A stellar reputation for producing earnings at times when they were hard to get, a showy lifestyle of cars, expensive works of art, and connections with celebrities, Madoff fooled investors; they had no idea that he was running an elaborate Ponzi scheme, moving money around to lead some of his clients to think they were making it when in fact they weren't because the money wasn't there.

He seemed to have hoodwinked so many mutual fund managers and celebrities that everyone was caught off guard by the crime. When the scheme was exposed, French hedge fund manager René-Thierry Magon de la Villehuchet, killed himself in his Manhattan office, having lost $1.4 billion of his clients' money to Madoff.

Out of the $36 billion invested with Madoff, the amount of his fraud was estimated to be between $12 billion and $20 billion. His reputation was in tatters for having stolen his clients' money (and causing the suicide of one man). Even under house arrest, he was mailing jewelry, watches, and other valuables to friends. His wife agreed to surrender $80 million worth of assets, keeping a measly $2 million for herself.

Madoff is scheduled to be released from prison in November, 2159.

Marc Dreier was a big player in the New York legal scene and the only equity partner of Dreier LLP. He went to Yale and Harvard. He had dapper suits. He owned a Picasso, a Warhol, and a big boat. Flouting his New York pedigree, he showed up at the offices of the Ontario Teachers' Pension Plan (OTPP) in Toronto and, as the police report alleges, used a meeting room at OTPP's offices to flog bogus securities pretending to be someone else (an activity that led to charges of personation under the *Criminal Code of Canada*, three nights in jail, and, I should add, the cancellation of the Dreier LLP Christmas party.

After posting bail in Toronto and flying back to New York, Dreier was immediately arrested and charged with fraud calculated at $100 million. The law firm that he named after himself (which had seven offices and staffed 300 people) blew up so fast, no one was left to take the firm's website down for a month. Apparently, some of the firm's trust funds mysteriously went missing and the firm's lawyers' liability insurance wasn't paid.

Dreier pleaded guilty to the criminal charges and was sentenced to 20 years' imprisonment. The US Securities and Exchange

Commission filed a separate civil suit against him for stealing funds from an escrow account belonging to one of his law firm's clients. As well, he was charged with money laundering and having sold $700 million worth of bogus securities.

As a lawyer myself, I predict that the name Dreier will enter the English legal lexicon in the same manner that Charles Ponzi's name became synonymous with "Ponzi" schemes and Vidkun Quisling's name became shorthand for "traitor." It's only a matter of time before the phrases "going for a spin in the Dreier" and "hung out to Dreier" become famous!

The whole affair was slightly (though not so criminally) reminiscent of the merger between the Toronto law firm Torys and New York firm Haythe & Curley around 1999. As the ink was drying on the merger contracts, named New York partner Tom Haythe was reported to have sexually harassed one or more of his new female colleagues at a party celebrating the merger, leading to his very hasty resignation from the firm and a quick branding change to remove his name from all signage, letterhead, and firm history. Tory Haythe became Torys.

Martha Stewart, homemaker extraordinaire, television personality, multimillionaire writer, and Martha Stewart Living Omnimedia publisher was indicted by a US federal grand jury on nine counts involving insider trading. She was alleged to have sold shares of ImClone Systems Inc. after receiving an illegal, inside tip that a cancer drug ImClone was testing would not be approved for sale. Her dumping of 4,000 ImClone shares before the rest of the world knew the shares would be worthless saved her $51,000 USD. She was convicted of one charge of conspiracy, one charge of obstruction of justice, and two charges of making false statements to investigators. She was sentenced to five months in prison, five months' home confinement, and two years' probation.

Baron Black of Crossharbour, sometimes known as Lord Black, born Conrad Black, and former inmate 18330-424 in the Coleman Federal Correctional Complex, in Florida, was a newspaper baron who owned such papers as the *Chicago Sun-Times*, *The Daily Telegraph*, *The Jerusalem Post*, and the *National Post*, and gave up his Canadian citizenship to become a British Lord.

He counted as his friends and colleagues Margaret Thatcher and Henry Kissinger. With houses in Palm Beach, New York, and London, his showy lifestyle came crashing down when he was convicted of offenses relating to securities fraud and obstruction of justice. He was discovered on a security video removing 13 boxes of financial documents out the back door of his Toronto office despite a court order requiring him not to do so, something that was not only posted on YouTube, but was pivotal in the jury trial that convicted him of obstruction of justice, lending credence to the adage that a "picture is worth a thousand words." That picture (or more correctly, that video) has been seen by millions of people. At the time of writing, he was released on bail pending a retrial on a matter relating to his conviction.

Sarah the Duchess of York, the former Sarah Ferguson, married and was then divorced by Prince Andrew around the same time tabloids featured compromising pictures of her, and her toe, with a wealthy American financier.

In 2010, Ferguson was secretly filmed by the *News of the World*, a London tabloid, promising access to her ex-husband Prince Andrew, for £500,000. She accepted a briefcase with $40,000 in it and said "500,000 pounds, when you can, to me ... open doors" on a video of the sting. "Look after me and he'll look after you," she said. The royal editor of *News of the World*, Robert Jobson, stated in an interview with the BBC that "What is very serious here is that she's so desperate that she's prepared to jeopardize the reputation of her ex-husband and of the country, and of an important international ambassadorial role, which is, after all, funded in terms of the expenses by the taxpayer." Now if that doesn't ruin a reputation, I'm not sure what would.

Senator John Edwards of North Carolina was a first-rate trial lawyer before he entered the US Senate in 1998. With a handsome "Kennedy-esque" demeanor, and excellent oratory skills, it wasn't all that surprising that he would seek higher office. He was Senator John Kerry's running mate in the Presidential Election of 2004, and ran for the Democratic Presidential nomination in 2008.

Edwards' campaign floundered, in part because of rumors of an extramarital affair he had with a campaign assistant while his wife was being treated for breast cancer. Edwards denied the affair, and denied the paternity of his mistress' child. He went so far as to have another campaign aide, Andrew Young, claim that he, not Edwards, was the child's father despite the fact that Edwards always knew that he was the child's father.

Young inevitably published a tell-all book where he described how he was tasked with setting up private meetings between Edwards and his mistress, and that Edwards promised his mistress that when his wife died, they would get married on a rooftop in New York City with the Dave Matthews Band playing at the wedding. In his book, and in TV interviews, Young revealed that not only was he asked to take responsibility for the child's paternity so that Edwards could keep campaigning without the stain of a sex scandal, but Edwards went so far as to tell Young to arrange for a doctor to "fake the DNA results" and to steal a diaper from the baby so he could do a DNA test to find out if the baby was his.

In the corporate world, we need go no further than banks and investment houses (and of late, one particular oil company that couldn't seem to shut down an oil well blowout a mile under the Gulf of Mexico) to see how bad decisions, bad timing, or bad behavior can detrimentally effect a corporate reputation and ruin a brand. A list of all failed US banks can be found on the Federal Deposit Insurance Corporation's (FDIC) website (http://www.fdic.gov/bank/individual/failed/banklist.html).

2. Case Studies

The following case studies are some famous online reputation management problems and how some companies dealt with them (or didn't deal with them).

2.1 Case Study 1: United Airlines

Sometimes, a company really deserves bad publicity.

Halifax band Sons of Maxwell were on tour in 2008, traveling by airplane from Halifax to Nebraska via Chicago. Musician, Dave Carroll, overheard the woman behind him on the plane say, "My God, they're throwing guitars out there." Carroll's bass player looked through the plane's window and saw the United Airlines baggage handlers throwing his guitar off the plane.

Caroll told *CBC News* that he tried to alert at least three employees at the time about the guitar being thrown, but they apparently showed no interest. Carroll's $3,500, 710 Taylor acoustic guitar had been custom-made for him and was packed in a padded double case so it would survive a flight, but it was smashed. Of course, United Airlines refused to take responsibility for the damage. Carroll told *CBC News* that he sent emails, wrote letters, and talked to people at United over a nine-month period until a United Airlines employee told him to "stop sending emails because you aren't going to get compensation."

Said Carroll, "What would Michael Moore do if he was a singer-songwriter?" Carroll decided to write three songs about his misadventure with United Airlines, and posted videos of the first song on YouTube. The song laments (in the way only a country and western song would lament) about helplessly watching from the plane as his guitar was thrown and destroyed.

The video went viral and had 150,000 hits in its first day. It had been seen 1.5 million times within four days of posting and by mid-2009 had been viewed more than 4.3 million times. In July, 2010, as I write this, it had been viewed more than 9 million times on YouTube (which doesn't include other web-based platforms where it may also have been seen).

After the video went viral during the first week, United Airlines made an attempt to make good by offering a $3,000 donation to the Thelonious Monk Institute of Jazz. (Note that Carroll is not a jazz player, so why United didn't do their research strikes me as a good reason to fire their PR department). It seemed to be a feeble public relations stunt.

A few days after the song went online, the bad PR for United caused its stock price to suffer. *The Times* in London reported the stock had "plunged by 10 percent costing shareholders $180 million." *The Times* went on to say that total "would have bought Carroll more than 51,000 replacement guitars."

United Airlines spokeswoman Robin Urbanski issued a press release about the incident:

"This has struck a chord with us. We are in conversations with one another to make what happened right, and while we mutually agree that this should have been fixed much sooner, Dave Carroll's excellent video provides United with a unique learning opportunity that we would like to use for training purposes to ensure all customers receive better service from us."

Carroll told *CBC News* he'd hoped his song was going to make a difference for people whose luggage is damaged by airline personnel.

"They're talking about changing the culture of customer service. This could end up making a real difference," he said to the CBC.

"United Breaks Guitars" made it to the number one country song on iTunes' download chart for the UK. Meanwhile, Taylor Guitars (being the brand of the guitar owned by Carroll and damaged by United), had immediately offered to replace the guitar and became the recipient of considerable positive media attention at the expense of United Airlines. If United were the villains in the song, Taylor Guitars were the good guys with the white hats.

What's the lesson to be learned from this story? Advertisers and marketers will readily use viral marketing avenues like Facebook and YouTube to promote a new product or service; however, disgruntled and upset consumers can also engage in viral marketing campaigns of their own if they're suitably motivated. Poor product reviews and horrible experiences with a company can spread virally, especially involving businesses that consumers "love to hate" such as airlines, banks, law firms, the medical profession, and other industries where consumers might think, rightly or wrongly, that they're getting ripped off.

PR executives, social media experts, and even lawyers now admit that businesses which don't treat their customers well, or don't react to customer service complaints in a fair and timely manner, will suffer the wrath of consumer-powered YouTube and Facebook revolts. Disgruntled consumers with a lot of anger and a little free time will happily post an embarrassing video on YouTube, or create a critical Facebook group, or take other actions online to shame and embarrass a business that caused them the pain.

Who needs lawyers anymore when the "Court of Public Opinion" can have immediate and lasting results? If you think the broken guitar is an isolated event, one passenger on a Delta flight posted a YouTube Video called "Delta Flight 6499, SEVEN HOURS on the tarmac."

Now, more than ever before, companies don't own brands: consumers do.

2.2 Case Study 2: Domino's Pizza

It may have been just another week in the life of the Domino's Pizza franchisee, Kevin Hendren, in Conover, North Carolina, but the second week of April in 2009 was a week from hell for him and the Domino's system as a whole. One employee filmed another employee making a sandwich. The sandwich maker put cheese up his nose, then put the cheese (with nasal mucus) in the sandwiches together with some other actions best left to the imagination. The employee filming the event provided narration, and the video was posted to YouTube. How the person making the sandwiches or the one doing the filming thought they wouldn't be exposed is beyond understanding.

Within three days of the event, the video had been viewed more than a million times and references to the "Domino's video" were in 5 of the 12 top results on the first page of Google search for "Domino's." Commentary about the disgusting Domino's video had spread throughout Twitter and on blogs. The employees, who filmed and posted the activity, told Domino's representatives (and later, the police) that they had never actually delivered the food and that it was a prank.

Kristy Hammonds and Michael Setzer, the Domino's employees in the video, were promptly fired, and criminally charged with delivering prohibited foods. The local health authority, which was brought in after the matter went public, required that all open food in the kitchen be discarded. This may have been the smallest damage caused by these individuals. They're also now being sued in a civil lawsuit by Domino's and the franchisee.

Said a Domino's public relations spokesperson to *The New York Times* in an article published April 15, 2009: "We got blindsided by two idiots with a videocamera and an awful idea. Even people who've been with us as loyal customers for 10, 15, 20 years, people are second-guessing their relationship with Domino's, and that's not fair."

In a matter of 72 hours, Domino's reputation was horribly damaged. The *New York Times* reported that a survey performed by YouGov (the company surveys close to 1,000 consumers each day regarding various brands) after the incident looked at Domino's reputation and reported that its reputation for quality among consumers had gone from "positive" to "negative," all because of the YouTube event.

How did Domino's react? Arguably, poor at first. If you don't have a presence in social media, it may be difficult to understand how fast a negative event or critical comment can catch a company by surprise and circulate virally to millions of people, before the company in question has any idea what has happened. When the problem was discovered, Domino's published an apology in print media, and did interviews on TV and radio. Patrick Doyle, President of Domino's USA posted his own apology on You Tube (http://www.youtube.com/watch?v=dem6eA7-A2I).

Did Doyle's apology work?

One anonymous comment to Doyle's apology video stated that he or she would never order food that wasn't prepared right in front of his or her face. The person also added that he or she wouldn't be going to Domino's again.

Sadly, only 13,000 people actually watched Patrick Doyle's apology on YouTube despite *The New York Times* reporting that the "prank" had been viewed more than a million times on YouTube within 72 hours of it being uploaded. Clearly, even a heartfelt apology to customers wasn't as sensational as the disgusting prank itself. The Domino's franchise owner who owned the location where the incident occurred closed his business in September, 2009. "My business was off 58 percent because of YouTube," Kevin Hendren said to *Hickory Daily Record*.

"Try as he might, the franchisee couldn't get enough people to come back and the store was no longer viable," said Tim McIntyre, a spokesperson for Domino's. Referring to the two former employees, "In their attempt to be funny, they left a lot of victims in their wake — the business owner, 20 of their fellow coworkers who are now out of work, community groups that benefited from the store's outreach programs, on and on."

What is the lesson here? Unlike the United Airlines video discussed in section **2.1**, where a company wasn't accepting responsibility for its actions (and arguably deserved all the YouTube exposure it got), Domino's and its franchisee really weren't to blame for the disgusting activities of two entry-level employees with a videocamera and no common sense. Setzer was given a 6-month suspended sentence and 24 months of supervision after pleading guilty in March 2010 to adulterating food.

What could Domino's have done better? First, if the franchisee had a policy respecting YouTube and other social media as part of its employment contract, and an agreement that a violation of that policy could mean termination of an employee and potential legal action for damages, it's possible the employees might have thought twice before creating and posting their video. I said possible, not probable, because you can't prevent stupidity, even contractually.

The real thing that Domino's could have done better may have been to monitor their brand online with dedicated personnel looking for how the brand was being referred to online. They may well have detected the Internet chatter about the video a day or two before they did. Using a service such as Google Alerts (discussed in Chapter 9) might have given Domino's a head start in realizing the problem and reacting to it quicker.

For all of us, the Domino's Pizza video serves as a wake-up call for the following reasons:

- Never underestimate the power of social media to help or hurt your brand and reputation. Good and bad stories can be seen by millions of people in a matter of days, if not hours. The problem is, the bad ones spread like wildfire. The good ones don't.

- Companies must constantly monitor their online reputation to see what is being said about them in the traditional media, in blogs, on Twitter, on Facebook, on YouTube, and anywhere else on the Web where one comment or image can have a serious detrimental impact. Use Google Alerts or another service every day to see what is being said about your business online. Domino's couldn't prevent this, but if they had more notice, they might have been able to deal with the crisis faster and diffuse it better.

- Have a crisis management plan in effect to deal with online public relations crises. There are PR and marketing professionals that can help formulate such a plan.

- Be proactive on the web. Understand that millions of eyes which used to be reading the paper or watching TV are now on the Web looking at YouTube videos and Facebook posts that may be about you or your brand.

- Have social media policies in place with your employees as a part of their terms of employment that make it clear that if your brand is disparaged by them online, legal consequences will occur beyond mere firing. (But make sure they read the "firing" bit.)

2.3   Case Study 3: The Royal Canadian Mounted Police (RCMP)

On October 14, 2007, Robert Dziekański boarded a flight in Poland that would take him to Vancouver. He had planned to immigrate to Canada and live with his mother, Zofia Cisowski, in Kamloops, BC.

Dziekański had never flown before, and he could not speak English. His plane was late and after he completed initial immigration processing, his whereabouts between 4:00 p.m. and about 10:45 p.m. in the secure and controlled areas of Vancouver International Airport are not known. At some point, cameras caught him near baggage carousels. At other points during the night, people remember seeing him. Dziekański's mother had told him to wait for her after he had cleared immigration near the public area of the airport where baggage was picked up. But he was in a "secured area" as he hadn't been cleared for release from immigration, and she was in a public area, unable to see him or otherwise contact him.

Later that night, when he attempted to leave the Customs area, he was told to proceed to "secondary immigration" as his visa had not yet been fully processed, and by midnight, Dziekański's immigration was completed. After approximately a half hour in an immigration holding area, he was moved to the international arrivals reception area. Meanwhile his mother had been asking airport personnel throughout the afternoon as to the whereabouts of her son, but staff stated her son was not at the airport so she assumed he had missed his flight. She returned home to Kamloops.

When Mr. Dziekański left the Canada Customs area, he became quite angry and agitated.

Remember, Mr. Dziekański had landed at 3:00 p.m. (the plane was two hours late arriving in Vancouver), and he was likely exhausted, hungry, and jet lagged. Other passengers and airport security could not communicate with him because he couldn't speak English. So in an agitated state, and for unknown reasons, he used chairs to prop open doors between a Customs holding lounge and a public lounge, and he threw a little table on the ground.

The RCMP arrived, and we know more about the events of the next five minutes because another passenger collecting his luggage, Paul Pritchard, recorded what happened next on video. Because of Pritchard's video of the events, which later went public, this may be one of the best examples of an online (and offline) reputation management disaster, bringing the high reputation of the RCMP into distrust and disrepute.

Four RCMP officers entered the Customs room where Dziekański was standing. They ordered him to stand near a counter, and Dziekański moved, but for some reason he picked up a stapler off the desk. Within 30 seconds after arriving, Dziekański was shot with a Taser, an electronic stun device that fires a 50,000-volt charge into a target, by one of the officers. Convulsing and screaming in pain, he fell to the ground and was tasered again, at which point the four RCMP officers pinned him down on his chest and placed handcuffs on his wrists behind his back. The third and fourth taser charges were fired at the same time just before Dziekański fell. Authorities investigating the incident determined he was tasered a total of five times. He screamed before he stopped moving. Although one of the officers stated he checked for a pulse, and found his heart had stopped, testimony from the other RCMP officers stated they never saw anyone checking for a pulse. Dziekański did not receive CPR until paramedics arrived on the scene 15 minutes later. They were unable to revive him and he died at the airport.

We might never have known all the facts about this tragic incident if Pritchard, the passenger waiting to have his luggage cleared, hadn't videoed the incident. We only know it took less than 30 seconds before the first taser shot was fired because you can count the seconds on the video from when the officers first arrived.

Pritchard, who filmed the event, offered his camera and the video to the RCMP, and the RCMP told him that they would return the camera and video within 48 hours. However, they only returned the camera with a new memory card and not the video that was taken by Pitchard, who repeatedly demanded it back. The RCMP did not return it (or for that matter, make a copy to return to him) until Pritchard made a court application to obtain the return of his property. This was one month after the incident. The RCMP argued that they kept the video to preserve the "integrity of the investigation," although one wonders why they simply didn't make a copy and give it to Mr. Pritchard when they said they would. A by-product of this sad story may well be that bystanders don't offer up videos filmed at a crime scene because they don't trust the police to return their property.

If the incident itself led to grave concern about the behavior of Canada's national police force, the video of it led to outrage around the world. It was broadcast on news channels worldwide, and on You-Tube; this, only two and a half years before Vancouver was to welcome the world to the 2010 Winter Olympics. A Commission of Inquiry was established to investigate the death of Dziekański, headed by retired Judge Thomas Braidwood, who held hearings for 70 days, where he heard contradictory testimony between what the officers said after the incident and what they said on the stand. The officers could be charged criminally for their actions, and this would never have come to light if a video of the incident hadn't been filmed.

The lesson for any police force in the world is that anyone with a cell phone can become a citizen-journalist and can (and will) film you doing your job, interacting with people, and making arrests. Some of these videos will be purchased by news organizations for lucrative prices, especially when there is an element of police brutality or other activity that oversteps what the public believes the officer ought to have done in the circumstances. Some police forces in the UK and US are now using headcams where all actions of the officer are recorded and retained on small hard drives within the camera; the video being used as evidence against a suspect, and perhaps, the officer as well.

As for the person filming the video? It seems that if you're going to offer the RCMP the video you just took of a police incident, you'll probably have to seek a court order to get it back.

2.4 Case Study 4: The teachers and the pep rally

Pep rallies can be career limiting, as two high school teachers in Winnipeg, Manitoba, found out in 2010. The teachers at Winnipeg's Churchill High School got carried away with the moment, and performed a raunchy and suggestive lap dance at a student pep rally in front of 100 students. The fully clothed performance included mock spanking and graphically implied oral sex. A student with a cell phone filmed it and posted it the next day to YouTube, resulting in the suspension and subsequent dismissal of the teachers involved.

The lesson here is abundantly clear. Although students might get a reprimand or a short suspension for such an activity (and celebrities and sports stars might get 60 seconds on *Entertainment Tonight*), if you're a teacher, or otherwise work with children or teens, you'll get fired for a lapse in judgment like this.

Winnipeg trustee Mike Babinsky told the *The Globe and Mail*, "It's unfortunate that this situation happened. A minute and a half of inappropriate dancing decided the fate of a big career change."

Said school board chair, Jackie Sneesby, about the matter, "I think most people know how to behave, and when we hire people they're expected to behave in a responsible way."

The lesson here? Teachers are on display 24/7. In these days of videocameras in cell phones, be assured that any lapse in judgment will be filmed and put on YouTube by students, and the person suffering the consequences will be the teacher.

If you're a teacher, you're already being scrutinized minute-by-minute by your students. Most students have cell phones and most cell phones have video and camera capabilities. You may be their teacher, but they are the new paparazzi, and you are Britney Spears or Ben Affleck.

2.5 Case Study 5: Ed Hardy

Ed Hardy is one of the many fashion brands of designer Christian Audigier. Almost every piece of clothing has a tattoo-inspired design; skulls with surfboards crashing out of temples; octopuses' tentacles peeping through the eyes and ears of the skulls. The Ed Hardy line of men's and women's clothes is not to everyone's taste. But some people like it or have worn it, including Britney Spears, Tara Reid, Paris Hilton, and Zac Efron. More than 680,000 people "like" the Ed Hardy Facebook fan page.

However, not everyone is a fan of Ed Hardy. "Thanks to Ed Hardy, now I can recognize a moron a mile away" and similar Facebook pages have been created by non-fans of Ed Hardy designs. In November 2009, a predecessor "Thanks Ed Hardy ... " Facebook page had 58,000 fans. Fans were encouraged to take pictures of people wearing Ed Hardy clothes, or find pictures on the Web of people wearing Ed Hardy clothes and comment, very disparagingly, about them.

Although the original "Thanks Ed Hardy ... " group page was removed from Facebook because the comments violated Facebook's terms of use (and were arguably defamatory), other, tamer groups have sprung up, such as "Thanks to Ed Hardy, I recognize idiots with no sense of style."

The lesson? Notoriety may be good for business, to a point. Perhaps you just let people rant for a while, at least until you get some press about it.

2.6 Case Study 6: Asleep at the switch

In January 2010, the Toronto news media was abuzz with the story about a Toronto Transit Commission (TTC) worker sleeping on the job. George Robitaille was a ticket collector for the TTC. Not only was he caught napping by some riders, he was photographed napping on the job behind the counter. A TTC customer made Robitaille instantly famous by taking a photograph of the sleeping conductor with his cell phone and posting it online. The photographer, Jason Wieler, said that he'd watched Robitaille dozing with his head back and his hands on his lap for five minutes. Outraged passengers wrote letters to the editor of Toronto's major newspapers demanding that the sleeping ticket taker be fired. Others in Toronto posted their own pictures of TTC employees sleeping on the job. Apparently, it was common.

The lesson? Again, almost every cell phone is a camera. If you fall asleep at the job, expect someone will take your picture and either post it on Facebook or send it to the local newspapers and television stations. If you're perceived to work in a cushy job with good pay, lots of benefits, a nice pension, and "banker's hours" (especially if that job is in the public sector), you'd better expect that anyone with a cell phone will try to make you famous for *not* doing your job.

2.7 Case Study 7: The candidate

Unfortunately, once a photo is on the Web (and Facebook in particular), it's there forever; and with some hunting, it can be found and recopied by anyone and everyone. This was a lesson learned by British Columbia New Democratic Party (NDP) candidate Ray Lam during the BC provincial election campaign of 2008, when some inappropriate photographs of him touching the private body parts of a woman were found on a Facebook page. He was forced to drop out of the election a few weeks before the vote after the pictures went public, and the NDP was forced to find a new candidate at the last minute in the middle of the election. That candidate lost.

The lesson here isn't for Lam, who allowed the photo to be taken in the first place, and either posted it to his Facebook page himself or allowed another person to post it to his or her page. It's really a lesson for the political party that allowed Lam to stand for election without thoroughly checking his online reputation first. All political candidates for any office should have their online reputations scrutinized by the party nominating them, because you can be sure the other political parties will be doing their own online audit of the opposing candidates come election time, and they'll make sure the "online bomb is dropped" during the election, not before.

If you're in a political party that is fielding candidates for an election, don't rely on your candidate to disclose whether there's anything embarrassing in his or her past that might embarrass the party or the candidate. Vet the candidate on Google. Require prospective candidates to allow access to their blogs, writings, Facebook pages, LinkedIn pages, and other social networking sites, because in an election, you have to know the other side will be doing it as well, and be looking to exploit any weakness a candidate has.

If you're a politician (or an aspiring one), and have some embarrassing photos of yourself, don't post them to Facebook and don't email them to others. The pictures will find their way to the media, perhaps ending your political career. If you're posting these photos to Facebook, maybe you shouldn't be a politician in the first place!

2.8 Case Study 8: The Russian policeman and YouTube

Alexei Dymovsky was a policeman in Novorossiysk and oversaw crimes related to drug trafficking. Upset with the bribery and corruption all around him, which led to the arrests of innocent people to satisfy a quota of arrests, he aired his grievances on YouTube in a series of videos he recorded in 2009. "I am not afraid," he explains, "I am telling my name … But I cannot stand detecting the nonexistent crimes, imprisoning people who are not guilty. I can't stand it anymore." His videos were viewed by millions of people in Russia.

The lessons here? Aggrieved employees and whistleblowers now have a digital soapbox to stand on to tell a worldwide audience about an organization and its shortcomings, whether or not those shortcomings are true or inflated. If your organization has embarrassing secrets or skeletons in its closet (even wrongdoings or crimes), a disgruntled employee armed with this information may well expose it all on YouTube to take revenge.

Here's a lesson for the whistleblowers of the world: Dymovsky was fired, then arrested, held in prison for months, and charged with fraud and abuse of office, which carries a prison sentence of up to ten years. Drugs were planted in his apartment to frame him and he was beaten up by his former coworkers (all police, by the way). The lesson is this, especially in corrupt countries where the legal protection for free speech is not as enshrined as it is in the United States, Canada, and Western Europe: You may be risking your personal safety by going on YouTube to expose the wrongdoings (real or imaginary) of your superiors and coworkers.

4
A LESSON IN BRANDING AND REPUTATION MANAGEMENT

In the mid-1990s I received an email from my brother, which he'd received from someone else, whom I can only presume received it from someone else in a long chain of "someone elses." It was the story of the Neiman Marcus Cookie recipe.

Neiman Marcus is a high-end clothing retailer in the United States, and in some of its locations, there are high-end restaurants. A woman and her daughter were eating in a Neiman Marcus restaurant in Dallas, and ordered a cookie for dessert. They loved the cookie so much, the mother asked for the recipe and she was prepared to pay $2.50 for it, because the server said it would cost "two fifty" to sell her the recipe. After seeing she was charged $250 for it on her Visa a month later, she decided to take revenge and make the recipe public so Neiman Marcus wouldn't make money off of it. She sent the recipe by email to hundreds of friends, acquaintances, and coworkers and asked them to send it to all of their friends, acquaintances, and coworkers. The recipe, once worth $250, was now worth nothing, because it had been spread virally around the world by a disgruntled customer.

This story is interesting for a number of reasons; chief among them is that it appears the consumer has finally found a way to stick it to the big voracious corporation. The problem is the story isn't true.

Neiman Marcus didn't have a chocolate chip cookie at the time the email went into wide circulation, and the company didn't take Visa at that time either. Neiman Marcus subsequently published a cookbook including the cookie recipe and made the recipe public.

The Neiman Marcus cookie recipe story is and always was a hoax, based on a similar hoax involving a cake recipe at the Waldorf-Astoria Hotel in New York in the 1940s. At one time, the hoax even appeared as the "Mrs. Fields' Cookie Recipe" story.

When people read this email, the first thought that may come to mind is that Neiman Marcus was a greedy, money-hungry retailer who got what it deserved for taking advantage of one of its consumers. The second thought may be, good job by the middle-class mom who stuck it to the big bad corporation and got revenge through her use of this wonder of mass communication: email.

Now that we know it was always a hoax, there's a third thing we should realize. A negative comment can seriously damage a brand. The comment can be started anywhere, for any reason, and can travel virally through the Web reaching millions of people, including consumers and potential consumers, in a matter of days (if not minutes). It can happen to any business.

These days, it can happen by viral emails, just like the Neiman Marcus cookie hoax. It can happen through online reviews and forums. It can come from bloggers, some of whom may try to hide behind the cloak of anonymity. And it can appear on social networking sites like Facebook.

1. Places Consumers Search Online for Reviews

Who makes these kinds of negative comments? Some of these comments can come from dissatisfied customers with an axe to grind, or competitors trying to discredit you and your business. Some of these comments can even come from your current or past employees, thinking they're getting even with you over a grievance. Some can come from websites or Facebook fan pages that are created simply to trash you and your brand.

If you're looking for a hotel in Istanbul, Athens, or Cairo, and haven't got a clue where to stay because you've never been there (and don't want to use a travel agent), TripAdvisor is a great source of information to help you make your decision. But a plethora of bad reviews (e.g., noisy street, rude staff, small rooms, "hotel staff didn't help me when the cab driver was rifling through my luggage") isn't going to endear you to stay at that hotel, is it?

Likewise, if you're looking for a doctor, you can look him or her up on RateMDs.com, RateMyMD.ca, DoctorScorecard.com, and other similar sites where patients themselves post positive or negative comments online about experiences they've had with a doctor. But are the comments legitimate? Consider whether the posters are "posers," not patients. Maybe one of them is someone who once worked for the doctor, or with the doctor. Or maybe it's the doctor's less-than-neighborly neighbor, who is having a dispute about a fence. Or perhaps there are a number of glowing, but anonymous comments that have been posted by the doctor (or his or her staff) to counteract a plethora of negative comments.

Looking for a new camera? If you want to see what others have to say about the camera you want, go to dpreview.com. That Chronoswiss Opus watch you saw in a window in Lugano, Switzerland? Find a review on watchreport.com. Want to buy a new book by your favorite author? Read the reviews on Amazon or Chapters/Indigo.

Of course, there are lots of sites where you can rate your lawyer (LawyerRatingz.com), professors and teachers, dentists, car mechanics, hairdressers, restaurants, and any other goods or services. Just use Google, ensuring the word "review" is used in the search box, and it will point you to a number of these kinds of sites where you can drill down deeper and read about (or review) all sorts of products, vendors, professionals, or service providers.

People talk online about you personally, about your company, and about your brand. Obviously, negative commentary online has an effect on your reputation and your brand's reputation.

Building and managing a brand and a corporate reputation has to take into effect sloppy journalism, talk radio, the curse of the 24/7 news cycle, "gotcha" watchdog interest groups looking for you or your brand to run into trouble, anonymous bloggers, and toxic online forum contributors, some of whom hide behind the cloak of anonymity. This doesn't even include crises in which a company can find itself.

As well, many companies, large and small, are asked to take public positions on anything from oil spills to solar energy to work-life balance to breastfeeding in public, and critics are there almost immediately to pounce on a company that deviates from another's social, political, or economic agenda. Some of these critics may in fact be competitors out to steal market share at the expense of your brand and reputation.

Let's spend some time on branding and reputation to convince you how important it is.

2. What Is a "Brand," and Why Is It Important?

If you're a listener of CBC Radio, as I am, you might recognize the name Terry O'Reilly. O'Reilly is what you might call an advertising and marketing guru. He's the cofounder of Pirate Radio and Television, a creative audio production company with studios in New York and Toronto. He's also the host of one of CBC radio's most interesting shows, "O'Reilly on Advertising" and "The Age of Persuasion." O'Reilly is a critic of our branded culture, but he's also a realist, and he knows about the importance of branding. This is how he describes what a brand is in the book he coauthored with Mike Tennant, *The Age of Persuasion: How Marketing Ate Our Culture*, published by Knopf Canada (2009):

"Branding is at the core of all marketing ... to me, it means defining what a product or service promises and how it differs from the competition. For example, Volvo is just a car, but when the idea 'safety' was added, its brand was defined. Nike is just a running shoe, but the powerful idea of 'personal achievement' was attached to every single advertising message they sent out, and that gave the famous footwear its own personality ... And then there's Coke. In a taste test, the iconic drink was compared to an undisclosed cola. People chose Coke over the mystery item almost a hundred to one. Then the undisclosed soda was revealed: it was in fact, Coke. The difference between the two was branding. The Coke enhances your life 'idea' beat the other cola, which had no idea attached to it. When people sampled Coke, they not only tasted the sugar and water combination; they also tasted the logo and the imagery, commercials, and promotions that have accompanied the drink for decades."

When a brand is associated with a product, a person, a company, or even a country, the "brand" creates value and "premiums" over and above what the "thing" the brand is attached to, and is otherwise worth. When you know its Coke, it's somehow more special than no-name cola, even if the no-name cola is Coke.

When I have to talk to someone about branding, I contact Michael Allabarton, now founding principal of BrandDig Consulting in Victoria, BC. Allabarton's been around the marketing and advertising business for more than 25 years, having worked with Malahat Group Communications, Palmer Jarvis DDB, and global agency BBDO.

"Brand is a nebulous term with a multitude of interpretations," Allabarton told me. "A brand is not just, as some may believe the culmination of a naming convention, logo, strap line, public relations, or endless adverting campaigns. Brand, and the act of branding, goes far deeper. Just as important to recognize is a company's brand value. Companies that understand the true meaning of brand value also understand they [the companies] do not own brands. Consumers do. Companies own trademarks."

Allabarton says, "Branding is the sum total of everything an organization does. Everything it stands for. Its values. Its behavior — the very thing that shapes the relationships a brand maintains with its audiences — both internal and external. Branding is an integrated personality and market positioning that projects the image and values of an organization. It's how a company reveals its personality and delivers on its consumer promise."

Allabarton also said that the principles of branding apply to all shapes and sizes of business entities whether it's a one-off storefront, a franchise, a large conglomerate, or even an individual, such as a high-profile athlete or politician.

Like it or not, Allabarton suggests we live and work in a branded culture — where people form real relationships with brands. These relationships are built on trust and maintained through fulfillment of expectations. He goes on to say that these expectations need to be perfectly aligned with a company's "consumer proposition," which is the promise an organization makes to its audiences. To be successful this promise must be delivered — consistently and throughout an organization — and consumers who experience this consistency are not only prepared to pay a price premium, they become willing advocates for a brand. It's at this stage in the process — brand advocacy — that the consumer-brand relationship is spot-welded.

Going back and forth with Allabarton over a series of emails and phone conversations, he explained to me that successful brands have integrity. They do what they say they're going to do. They make a promise and they live up to it. They walk the walk. So, going back for a moment to the importance of aligning customer expectations with a brand's promise, if the branding message is fragmented, its imagery confusing, or the performance of the brand is inconsistent with the promise, trust is diminished and a brand can become destabilized, even dysfunctional.

As mentioned, Allabarton suggests organizations that truly understand branding, and its importance, recognize that items such as logos, slogans, and advertising and public relations campaigns do not represent the construct of branding in its entirety. These are merely devices, or ways in which to articulate a brand's promise to consumers. These are tools — in a marketer's toolkit — that reach out to audiences and serve to distinguish one brand from another, by simply portraying, or acting out, its values and behavior.

Allabarton explains that labeling things such as campaigns and slogans as tools, or devices, isn't to suggest that they aren't valuable in building brand. They most certainly are. But they can also be the thin-edge-of-the-wedge. We've all been exposed to ad campaigns that promise something, but don't even come close to lining up with the customer's in-store experience. It's in these instances when slogans and campaigns can drive a stake in the heart of a brand. As Allabarton warns, "there can be a nasty downside to clever and attractive ad campaigns, intent on luring in customers. When attached to an underperforming brand, they only serve to accelerate its demise."

It's safe to suggest, therefore, that brand management is of paramount importance, which brings us back to the notion of behavior. In the context of a recognizable brand in, say the fast-food franchising industry, Allabarton says if a single franchisee is poorly managed and continually misbehaves — by not fulfilling its consumer or brand proposition, or accurately delivering brand value — it potentially impacts every franchisee within the group. For example, what if you have a bad experience at a McDonald's in Walla Walla, Washington; Woodburn, Oregon; or Beynac, France? Maybe it was an unclean restaurant? Or the staff was rude? Wouldn't this impact the view that a consumer may have about McDonald's in Vancouver, New York, or Toronto? You can bet if consumers have bad experiences at a restaurant anywhere in the world, McDonald's will be on top of the situation immediately. It has too much to lose.

Further to Allabarton's notion that branding is truly about behavior, let's look again to our discussion of Tiger Woods from Chapter 3. Allabarton told me the "Tiger Brand" simply misbehaved. It acted out of character, or "off brand." Woods' audience interpreted brand value one way, built a relationship based on this understanding, then punished the brand when it did not fulfill its collective expectations. It's safe to suggest that perhaps, at least in the case of Tiger Woods, the brand promise may have been a tad too lofty and too difficult to deliver, and it was probably too challenging to manage behavior consistent with such a promise. After all, Woods is only human.

If you want to drill deeper into the importance of brand, integrity, values, and reputation, pick up Peter H. Thomas' *Be Great: The Five Foundations of an Extraordinary Life in Business — and Beyond* (Wiley, 2009). Thomas was the founder and chairman of Century 21, a successful real estate franchise in Canada. He started at a time when national real estate franchises were few and far between in both the US and Canada.

Thomas has five core principles of value-based living, and these principles are applicable to people, companies, and to a large extent, brands:

1. **Values:** Clarify your personal, professional, and corporate values and live them, day by day.

2. **Focus:** Understand the power of focus and how to apply it, whether in your personal life, your business life, or the "life" of your company and the products and services it offers to the public.

3. **Visualization:** If you can picture your goal, you can work toward it. This applies to people as much as it applies to organizations.

4. **Inspiration:** Celebrate the genius within you.

5. **Reflection:** Tap into the positive forces that you control.

Fundamental to people and companies is your integrity. Thomas says, "If you have a set of principles that you live by, that includes personal and business integrity, it becomes your brand. It becomes who you are. Our integrity is tested every day. I have learned over the years that to consider all decisions can be thought of as being either black or white — yes or no — there is no gray. Usually when we are confronted with an integrity issue our hearts know what we should do but our brain has the capacity to rationalize. Go with what your heart says when issues come up that test your integrity — your heart does not rationalize."

3. Brands Aren't Trademarks

I speak a lot about branding in this book because of the interrelationship between branding and reputation in the corporate world, and the damage that can be done to brands and reputations from online activities. Trademarks are important because they are one of the main ways brands are protected under law.

If you find your brand has been tarnished by activity online, you might seek to have the Facebook status update, fan page, YouTube video, digital photograph, or other commentary removed because it infringes on, or otherwise interferes with, your trademark rights.

To be able to argue with YouTube, Facebook, and others that your trademark rights have been infringed, or interfered with, you'd better know what a trademark is.

In the United States and Canada, a trademark can be a word (e.g., Apple for computers, phones, and virtually everything else with an off switch); numbers (e.g., Lotto 6/49); slogans (e.g., We do it all for you.), and logos without words (e.g., Nike swoosh). It can even be a shape (e.g., the ubiquitous Coke bottle shape is a trademark known as a "distinguishing guise").

A trademark distinguishes your goods and services from the goods and services of others in the marketplace. Ideally, you'll want a trademark that's not barred from registration for technical reasons under the Lanham (Trademark) Act in the US, or the *Trade-marks Act* in Canada. You'll want one that's distinctive of you and your goods or services, and not one that is generic or is registered for so many different products and services by so many other vendors that it isn't distinctive. You'll especially want one that isn't confused with a trademark someone else owns (this could either be someone with a registered trademark for the same goods or services you plan to register for). Or it could be a user of a trademark who hasn't registered, but who has used it for longer than you have.

Trademark rights in the US and in Canada are generally determined by the first to *use*, not the first to register. You can apply for a trademark based on actual use (i.e., you can prove you've used it in respect of the sale of goods or the advertising or performance of services), or on the basis of proposed or intended use (i.e., you intend to use it within the next three or so years). You can use your application or registration in one country to apply for the same mark in other countries with certain priority benefits, which helps if you want to expand internationally.

As for trademark searches, before you spend your money applying for a trademark (or indeed, selling products or providing services under that mark), you should search your trademark to make sure no one else has the same name or logo, or one that is confusingly similar to yours. In Canada, navigate to the CIPO database at www.ic.gc.ca to search for a trademark. In the United States, navigate to TESS at http://tess2.uspto.gov. Note, however, that the searches you get from these public databases are not definitive, and you may well have to hire a trademark professional to further search your trademark.

4. Copyright

You might also take the position that information posted on a social networking site is an infringement of your copyright. Or alternatively, if you're the person posting to a social networking site, someone else may argue that what you have posted is an infringement of his or her copyright. Copyright is not just for novelists and musicians.

Copyright means, quite simply, the right to copy. Copyright provides protection for literary, artistic, dramatic, or musical works including computer programs, as well as performance, sound recording, and communication signals. Only the owner of copyright has the right to produce or reproduce a work or allow someone else to do that. Copyright is the right granted to the owner of a work to print, copy, or distribute a work or make a derivative version of the work (e.g., a film based on comic book, a TV show based on a novel). More important, copyright gives its owner the right to stop others from copying that work or a portion of it.

Copyright is simply the right to copy someone else's original work in a fixed form. It applies to the following types of works:

- Literary works, such as books, stories, poetry, text, and computer programs

- Dramatic works, such as film, DVDs, theatrical plays, and screenplays
- Musical works such as songs, with and without lyrics
- Artistic works such as paintings, drawings, photographs, sculptures
- Architectural works as well as maps, blueprints, compilations, and mortgage tables

The owner of copyright (who is not necessarily the original creator) has the right to prevent another party from making copies of that work. At its most basic, that's all copyright is. Of course, it is more complicated than that, which is why there are numerous textbooks, cases, case comments, and legal articles on the topic.

With the advent of technology, copyright extends to other matters such as the following:

- Sound recordings such as LPs, CDs, VHS, DVDs, and Blu-rays
- Communication signals (the electronic signals that are transmitted by broadcasters)
- Performances by actors, singers, dancers, and musicians

Copyright can be complicated. Some rights derive from other rights, and there are separate rights that you would not expect to be separate. For example, when you load a CD into your car stereo, there is copyright in the device (the CD itself) and also a copyright in a song. The recording of a song is one right; the song itself is another. They could be owned by different parties. One might think of copyright as a "pie" where the various neighboring and overlapping rights that could be held by performers, writers, musicians, broadcasters, and DVD manufacturers and distributors are sliced up.

When someone *owns* copyright, the **Copyright Acts** of the United States or Canada (the law in question depends on where you live), it gives the owner the rights to use and commercially exploit those rights. Bear in mind that many originators of artistic, literary, musical, or dramatic works no longer own the works they have created. Why? They have assigned their rights to publishers, music companies, film production companies, and other businesses that require ownership of the copyright to commercially exploit the product.

Authors and creators — unless they're successful and economically very powerful — will have assigned copyright to see their manuscript in print, hear their song on the radio, browse for their novel in a bookstore, or see their screenplay on the screen. The commercial world often requires many authors and creators of works to assign those works for commercial exploitation.

Ownership of the copyright in a work includes a number of other rights which you might not otherwise think of. For example, it includes the right to —

- convert a dramatic work into another kind of work, such as a novel;
- convert a novel into a dramatic work;
- publish a translation of a work;
- make a sound recording (e.g., an audio book) of a dramatic, musical, or literary work;
- reproduce, publicly present, and adapt a film;
- broadcast the work on TV or cable; and
- license computer programs.

Copyright has its limitations, though. It applies to songs, novels, plays, magazine articles, computer programs, and so on, but does not apply to plots or characters in a novel, factual information, the idea for a plot for a novel, or the title to a song, nor will it protect the name of a television show, book, or movie, although those might be protected through trademark law.

Someone who uses a copyrighted work without consent is said to be *infringing* on the owner's copyright. Infringement is actionable under copyright laws. There are, however, certain exceptions to infringement, such as the private performance of another person's song in your house or making a copy of a musical recording for private use.

Fair dealing/fair use allows people to quote works from books, articles, and other works for private study, research, or criticism, review, or news reporting. Infringement of copyright includes —

- the public performance of a theatrical play without consent of the owner of those rights,

- photocopying articles for distribution to students at a university or school without consent of the owner of those rights,

- video recording a concert without consent of the owner of those rights, and

- the mere reprinting of an article without consent of the owner.

Remember, fair dealing, as well as other aspects of copyright, are treated differently in the United States, in Canada, in the UK, and other countries. In the United States, you can access excellent information on copyright law and the policies and procedures of the US Copyright Office at www.copyright.gov. In Canada, the Canadian Intellectual Property Office's website is located at www.cipo.gc.ca, and you can navigate to the copyright section of the website.

4.1 How copyright may affect you or your business

The use of background music in an aerobics studio or a restaurant is subject to copyright, because someone else's music cannot be publicly played without consent, which usually means payment for use of the music. Restaurateurs, bar owners, and especially fitness studio operators are sometimes surprised to learn that they're required to pay a copyright collecting agency an annual tariff based on a formula derived from the number of seats in their establishments or members in their fitness clubs.

Here's another example. Small-business owners who engage advertising and design companies to create logos, artwork, and websites for the business may be surprised to learn that the copyright in the design and artwork is almost always retained by the design company that created it, not the business that paid for it to be done. Your written contract would have to have assigned the copyright in the designs, ad copy, and artwork to you for you to own the copyright. If you're concerned, maybe you want this assignment language in the contract you have with your agency.

Likewise, if your company has hired employees to create designs, ad copy, or other works, your company owns the copyright in their workers' product, unless of course they are contractors, not employees (in which case, unless a contract says otherwise, the contractors own the copyright in their work product, not you). If you're concerned, you should put something in the contract you have with your workers to formally establish your copyright ownership of the work.

A discussion of copyright must include the issue of *moral rights*. In Canada and other countries, the creator of a work, even though he or she may have sold copyright of a work, still maintains a "moral" right to the work, to prevent the work from being distorted, mutilated, or otherwise modified in a way that is prejudicial to the reputation of the work or the creator. The best example of this is the case of artist Michael Snow, who created flying Canada Geese sculptures for the Toronto Eaton Centre. The mall was forced to remove red Christmas bows from around the necks of the geese as they distorted his original work. However, copyright assignments often contain a waiver of the artist's moral rights. In the United States, moral rights are protected differently, through both state laws (such as in California and New York), and through the Visual Artists Rights Act.

Again, every country has different laws governing copyright, and the number of years that copyright is protected will differ, depending on the work and the country. Countries that have signed an international treaty called the Berne Convention automatically extend to authors from other signatory countries the same copyright protection they give their own nationals.

5
THE APOLOGY: SOMETIMES YOU HAVE TO SAY YOU'RE SORRY, AND MEAN IT

During his 2000 presidential campaign, George W. Bush called a reporter from *The New York Times* a "major league asshole" just before a campaign speech, but he didn't realize a microphone was on. Bush later apologized for his comments.

Bush didn't say, "I apologize for making those comments. It wasn't very presidential of me and I regret any embarrassment I may have caused to the reporter," or any other words that suggested that he was sorry for the remarks. What he did say was, "I regret that a private comment I made to the vice-presidential candidate made it onto the public airwaves. I regret everybody heard what I said."

Read it again, because it symbolizes the sort of apologies that politicians and others make to improve or salvage a reputation that has been damaged by something they've said or done. However, it's not an apology at all if he is not saying he's sorry and taking responsibility for his transgressions.

Bush regretted that everyone heard what he said, but did not regret what he said, which is an example of "spin doctoring" at its finest. He gives the impression of giving an apology, but doesn't apologize for the remarks. He apologized that the remarks were heard. It's a work of art, if your art is the art of spin, obfuscation, and deception.

1. Accepting Responsibility

The story of Maple Leaf Foods was not caused by something that was done online. However, it illustrates how to apologize when you or your company has done something horribly wrong.

In 2008, Maple Leaf Foods had a disaster on their hands due to an outbreak of listeriosis in its packaged meat products. Lunch meat manufactured and packaged in Toronto under the Burns and Maple Leaf brands was infected with the bacteria, and 22 people in British Columbia, Ontario, Quebec, and Saskatchewan who consumed the tainted meat died. Others who ate the meat but recovered are still putting their lives back together, as are friends and families of all those affected.

What is your company to do if illness or death is clearly caused by your products? Do you deny responsibility and let the lawyers fight it out in court? Do you spin, weave, dodge, or bob around the issue to avoid legal liability in hopes of saving the brand's reputation? Or do you listen to the lawyers and deny everything? Maple Leaf Foods chose to not listen to their lawyers, which may have saved them.

Maple Leaf Foods admitted it was their fault and that they were responsible. They didn't dodge the issue, or blame those who were sick, or blame the inspection agency charged with ensuring the safety of the meat. They said, in essence, "it's our fault and we're going to fix it." Press releases issued after the incident said:

"This week our best efforts delivering the highest quality, safe food have failed us. For that we are deeply sorry. We know this has shaken consumer confidence in us. Our actions will continue to be guided by putting their interest first."

Maple Leaf Foods came straight out and apologized. It wasn't a legally crafted apology, or wordsmithery to deny culpability. They apologized in every media. They didn't dodge their responsibility but dealt with it up front and center.

They also didn't hire a celebrity to deliver the apology, nor did they hire a blonde actress with very white teeth wearing a lab coat. The company CEO and President, Michael McCain, immediately became the voice and face of the apology and what the company was doing to ensure food from Maple Leaf was safe. McCain personally apologized in print, and in a video that was broadcast on television and on YouTube. Here's what McCain said:

"Going through the crisis there are two advisors I've paid no attention to. The first are the lawyers, and the second are the accountants. It's not about money or legal liability; this is about our being accountable for providing consumers with safe food.

This is a terrible tragedy. To those people who have become ill, and to the families who have lost loved ones, I want to express my deepest and most sincere sympathies. Words cannot begin to express our sadness for your pain."

When Maple Leaf knew the problem was their fault, they acted decisively, and transparently. They recalled more than 200 packaged meat brands (amounting to tens of thousands of individual packages) manufactured or packaged at the affected plant. In press releases, Maple Leaf Foods stated that they continued to actively meet with the Canadian Food Inspection Agency (CFIA) and Public Health Agency of Canada (PHAC), as well as meeting with external industry experts about food-safety protocols, before reopening the facility. They also gathered industry-leading experts to consult and advise them on several physical and operational enhancements. "We believe it is important to take these broader preventative actions to respond to this situation promptly, comprehensively, and in the best interests of our consumers."

One year after the tragedy, Maple Leaf Foods Inc. placed full-page ads in *The Globe and Mail*, the *Edmonton Journal*, *The Vancouver Sun*, and other Canadian newspapers to mark the one-year anniversary of the listeriosis outbreak. It was framed as a letter to consumers from McCain. The ads said Maple Leaf was committed to "becoming a global leader in food safety to prevent this kind of a tragedy from ever happening again." McCain added, "On behalf of our 24,000 employees, we promise never to forget."

By dealing with a crisis by taking responsibility for it, Maple Leaf Foods may well have saved its brand and the company's reputation. By telling consumers "sorry, it's totally our fault and we'll fix it," despite what lawyers might have advised, gave consumers the confidence they needed. Customers appreciate it when someone actually takes responsibility for a mistake rather than weaving around the issue to avoid legal liability.

At the end of 2008, McCain was named business newsmaker of 2008 by *The Canadian Press*, based on his handling of the listeria crisis.

"Obviously, I have the pinnacle of that accountability and act as the face of the organization, but this was a very dedicated, principled team of leaders, all 23,000 of them, and we acted together through this," McCain said in an interview with *The Canadian Press*. "We would be thankful if we can fully recover our business and we're optimistic we can earn that trust back from consumers, but these types of things rarely should be described in terms of success or similar adjectives, because this is just an outright tragedy. I think all 24,000 people in our organization felt that way about it, but equally had a resolve to make a terrible wrong right in some meaningful way."

David Dunne, a marketing professor at the University of Toronto's Rotman School of Management, was quoted in *Digital Journal*, "Maple CEO Business Newsmaker of the Year," in January 2009 as saying:

"A lot of what they did was technically perfect. I think they've done as much as could be done, and it's a real example to other companies that face crises. Most companies are way too slow to deal with these things and tend to hide and they're afraid of admitting responsibility and so on, so this is a real example of how to do it right."

In the same article, Peter Lapinskie of *The Daily Observer* in Pembroke, said "[McCain's] candor at a time when his contemporaries would have scurried behind spin doctors and legal eagles was a refreshing way to address a potentially devastating mistake. I actually trust the man!"

McCain's actions also revealed a business savvy because he didn't wait too long to respond to the situation. Indeed, rather than fighting this in the courts, Maple Leaf settled a series of class-action lawsuits out of court by agreeing to pay the victims of the outbreak $27 million.

"In the scheme of things," said Dunne to *The Canadian Press*, "the value of the Maple Leaf brand is worth way more than $27 million over time, so (I'm not surprised) they would settle this quietly and reasonably quickly so it wouldn't go to court."

2. Sincere Apologies

Perfect Apology is a website devoted to helping people and businesses to salvage reputations by understanding what an apology is, in what circumstances an apology should be made, and how to make the right apology. Its website is PerfectApology.com.

They provide advice on ways to apologize, how to apologize, and how to express remorse and regret by way of illustrations of good and bad apologies. There are also templates for users to adapt their own apologies. This site is a very a useful tool in helping to deal with a corporate or personal reputation that has been damaged. Perfect Apology suggests the following for the best practices for a business apology:

- Give a detailed account of the situation
- Acknowledge the hurt or damage done
- Take full responsibility
- Recognize your role or the company's role in the situation
- Include a statement of regret
- Ask for forgiveness
- Promise that it won't happen again
- Provide a form of restitution, if possible

In the United States, another "perfect apology" is the one given by JetBlue CEO David Neeleman, in reaction to a disastrous Valentine's Day when passengers on a JetBlue flight from New York to Cancún were kept on the plane for nearly nine hours due to a snowstorm, crew shift changes, and other problems. Throughout that day, numerous other JetBlue planes were also stranded, along with their passengers, on the tarmac, and JetBlue flights were canceled for four days.

Neeleman gave a public apology for the cancellations and admitted that JetBlue had "mismanaged the situation." He said he was "humiliated and mortified" by the numerous system failures and he promised that JetBlue would immediately introduce a "Customer Bill of Rights" offering compensation for such events in the future. The full apology is worth reading:

Dear JetBlue Customers,

We are sorry and embarrassed. But most of all, we are deeply sorry.

Last week was the worst operational week in JetBlue's seven-year history. Many of you were either stranded, delayed, or had flights canceled following the severe winter ice storm in the Northeast. The storm disrupted the movement of aircraft, and, more importantly, disrupted the movement of JetBlue's pilot and inflight crew members who were depending on those planes to get them to the airports where they were scheduled to serve you.

With the busy President's Day weekend upon us, rebooking opportunities were scarce and hold times at 1-800-JETBLUE were unusually long or not even available, further hindering our recovery efforts.

Words cannot express how truly sorry we are for the anxiety, frustration, and inconvenience that you, your family, friends, and colleagues experienced. This is especially saddening because JetBlue was founded on the promise of bringing humanity back to air travel, and making the experience of flying happier and easier for everyone who chooses to fly with us. We know we failed to deliver on this promise last week.

We are committed to you, our valued customers, and are taking immediate corrective steps to regain your confidence in us. We have begun putting a comprehensive plan in place to provide better and more timely information to you, more tools and resources for our crew members and improved procedures for handling operational difficulties. Most importantly, we have published the JetBlue Airways Customer Bill of Rights — our official commitment to you of how we will handle operational interruptions going forward — including details of compensation. We invite you to learn more at jetblue.com/promise.

You deserved better — a lot better — from us last week and we let you down. Nothing is more important than regaining your trust and all of us here hope you will give us the opportunity to once again welcome you onboard and provide you the positive JetBlue Experience you have come to expect from us.

Sincerely,

David Neeleman

Founder and CEO

A sincere apology may result in reduced legal exposure, especially for doctors. Medical mistakes are reputed to cause anywhere between 40,000 and 90,000 deaths a year in the US. Studies done by medical professionals in the US suggest that doctors who apologize for a medical error, rather than avoid responsibility, are more likely to be appreciated by the patient and the family for honesty and integrity and are less likely to be sued for their mistake.

However, lawyers and the medical insurance companies don't want a doctor put on the witness stand to admit that he or she apologized for anything. Lawyers, especially lawyers who try cases in front of juries, believe that an apology is akin to an admission of having done something wrong, and you don't want the jury to hear anything but perfection when a doctor is on the stand.

Perfect Apology states that "doctors are not typically sued for medical malpractice because they make a mistake, they are sued because they shirk responsibility for the error, fail to apologize, and/or refuse to offer fair compensation to the patients and family to ease their pain and anguish."

Perfect Apology quotes Dr. Jerome Buckley, a retired CEO of a medical insurer. He is quoted as saying that the medical profession has made "a grave error when we listened to defense attorneys who told us to abandon our patients after adverse events. This is the chief reason we have a medical malpractice crisis."

Perfect Apology goes on to say, "This risk management strategy doctors have been encouraged to adopt to avoid lawsuits — deny any wrongdoing and defend every aspect of the medical procedures used — inevitably increases the likelihood of a long, divisive, and very expensive lawsuit."

Susan Forbes, QC, is the Director of Insurance for the Lawyers Insurance Fund of the Law Society of British Columbia, states that "We have found that in malpractice claims against lawyers, a sincere apology by the lawyer signals accountability and adds an element of vulnerability that can pave the way to resolution. This is the case, even when, as sometimes, it is given late in the day. It demonstrates that the lawyer understands and empathizes with the claimant, and is a simple but effective reminder of their shared humanity."

Many jurisdictions in North America have Apology Acts that attempt to encourage apologies by making them inadmissible in a civil action. The Massachusetts statute reads "Statements, writings, or benevolent gestures expressing sympathy or a general sense of benevolence relating to the pain, suffering or death of a person involved in an accident and made to the person or to the family of such a person shall be inadmissible as evidence of an admission of liability in a civil action."

Similar, but not identical statutes have been enacted in many states in the US, although in some states, if the apology was also made in conjunction with an admission of fault, that admission of fault would be admissible, arguably defeating the purpose of the apology.

British Columbia's *Apology Act* was the first to be enacted in Canada. It goes beyond medical lawsuits, and applies to any matter. Like other statutes in Canada that were enacted after BC, it allows persons and companies to apologize, and that apology may contain an admission of responsibility, without the apology being admissible as evidence in civil court to prove liability.

A sincere apology is an important tool that should be considered in all public relations crises and all disputes where a reputation stands to be further damaged without one. Indeed, the Canadian government recently apologized for the internment during World War II of Japanese citizens and Canadians of Japanese decent. The government apologized for the Chinese Head Tax levied on Chinese workers to discourage immigration in the last century. It apologized for the Komagata Maru incident where a boat filled with Sikh immigrants was denied landing in Vancouver. First Nations members have been apologized to by the Canadian federal and provincial governments for sexual and other abuse suffered during the time native students were required to attend residential schools in Canada.

As expressed by Hiroshi Wagatsuma and Arthur Rosett, in their influential examination of apologies, "The Implications of Apology: Law and Culture in Japan and the United States," while there are some injuries and damages that can *never* be repaired just by an apology, there are others that can *only* be repaired by one.

When you've done something offline or online that affects others detrimentally, remember how important a genuine apology can be; not only for the reputation of the person (or people) you're apologizing to, but your own reputation as well.

6

YOUR RIGHT TO PRIVACY AND THE PROTECTION OF YOUR PERSONAL INFORMATION

Your personal information is everywhere, and may well be used by others for things you didn't contemplate when you provided it (if you actually did provide it at all). If you are communicating with others through the Internet in general or on social networks in particular, you may find there is more personal identifiable information about you online than you ever expected.

You regularly give businesses and other organizations your information when you apply for a credit card, book travel tickets, enter a contest, shop on the Web, donate to a good cause, subscribe to a magazine, buy a book online, identify books or recording artists you like, comment in an online forum, sign up for a dating service, buy something on eBay, and in a multitude of important and mundane activities you do on a day-to-day basis. You leave a digital trail of information. This information is valuable, which is why businesses and other organizations either want to use it or sell it to someone who can use it.

Various amounts of your information, from your name and address to your shopping habits; your reading habits; the movies you rent; your health information; and perhaps information that can reveal your race, your income, a disability, your sexual orientation, or the movies you rented from your last hotel stay, is stored in numerous databases throughout the world. Some of this is aggregated in the sense that the businesses or organizations that "own" this information aren't so much interested in "you," but in the buying habits of "people like you," who share the same zip or postal code, or have the same interests, income, or education. Some of it is also about you, and only you because they want "you" to buy their stuff. Your information could be used by businesses to try to sell you more of what they sell. Or your information could be sold to others so that they can sell you their products too.

It's undeniable that privacy has taken a new twist; first by the advent of Facebook, Twitter, and YouTube, as well as personal blogs, online dating services, and smart phones with cameras and video capabilities. Second, by the perception — mainly held by those younger than 25, and particularly those with more than 700 Facebook friends — that their privacy doesn't really matter so much, or it's an issue for older people.

This is all in addition to the ever-increasing ability of computers to collect, organize, analyze, aggregate, store, and mine vast amounts of data on people, and what people do with their lives, their money, and their time.

If you are so inclined, you can use Blippy to automatically publish your credit card purchases online so that your "Blippy followers" (similar to Twitter followers) can see what you bought and can "like" or "not like" your purchasing decisions, your taste, or what you paid for your gaudy Ed Hardy shirt with the skulls and the snakes.

You could use services such as Google Latitude to allow people to track where you are using their cell phones, which interfaces your location onto Google Maps or Street View so someone else can see what store you're shopping in, or what restaurant you're eating in. Although Google states that this will allow you to know where your friends are having a drink or shopping, if your spouse is caught in traffic, or that your loved one's plane has safely landed, Privacy International has described this and other services in less flattering terms as a "gift to stalkers, prying employers, jealous lovers, and obsessive friends."

How about Facebook Places, a new geo-locating application introduced in August 2010 that uses the GPS mapping functions of your smartphone to let your Facebook friends know exactly where you are by "tagging" your location, even if you're in a place you don't want others to know about Facebook itself says that "Places" allows you to "Easily share where you are, what you're doing, and the friends you're with right from your mobile. Check in and your update will appear on the Place page, your friends' News Feeds and your Wall. Tag the friends you're with so they can be part of your update. Appear in 'Here Now' to friends and others nearby who are also checked in. 'I'm just down the street!' Never miss another chance to connect when you happen to be at the same place at the same time. Browse status updates of friends checked in nearby."

Individuals have the technological ability as well as the inclination to disclose their own and the personal information of others online, and this begs the question, what can be done when one individual makes another individual's personal information available online without consent? What happens when your private information is released to someone else? Breaches can and do happen.

In the United States, the social networking site RockYou suffered a serious data breach when a hacker gained access to more than 32,000,000 user accounts and passwords that were stored in plain text, making it easy for the hacker to gather all this information quickly and without immediate detection. Even worse, when RockYou downplayed the breach of its privacy obligations, the hacker published a portion of the information he had retrieved that revealed RockYou stored user credentials for social networks and other partner sites. RockYou's site did not have reasonable security measures to ensure users' protection of personal information.

What the person, company, or organization does with that information, and what you do if that information has been improperly collected or wrongfully used, is of great importance to people who care about their personal information. It's time to take a general look at the concept of privacy and personal information, particularly in Canada, because the Canadian Privacy Commissioner has been instrumental in changing the way social networking sites such as Facebook collect and use data all around the world.

1. Privacy

Generally, privacy is an individual's right to determine when, how, and to what extent he or she will release his or her personal information. It's about the intimacy, identity, dignity, and integrity of the individual.

You could also say that privacy is control over knowledge about oneself. When a court assesses whether a privacy right was violated, the court generally asks whether the plaintiff (i.e., the person making the complaint that his or her privacy right was violated) was actually entitled to privacy. This involves an assessment of the nature and degree of privacy to which the person was entitled. It's easiest to think of a person's right to privacy as falling along a continuum or a spectrum where his or her right to privacy is the strongest in the person's own home and weakest when he or she is in a public space. This analysis centers on the plaintiff's *reasonable expectation to privacy* in the given circumstances.

Note that different laws regarding privacy apply in different jurisdictions. The following sections will describe the privacy law regimes in the United States and Canada in general terms.

1.1 Privacy laws

In the United States, "invasion of privacy" is a legal cause of action in cases where a party alleges a right to privacy, and this has been breached by the other. Generally, there are four categories of invasion of privacy:

- **Intrusion of solitude:** Physical or electronic intrusion into a person's private life.

- **False light:** The publication of facts which place a person in a "false light," even though the facts themselves may not be defamatory.

- **Public disclosure of private information:** That is, the dissemination of truthful private information that a reasonable person would find objectionable.

- **Appropriation:** The unauthorized use of a person's name or likeness to obtain some benefits (often a commercial benefit).

Although the word "privacy" is actually never used in the text of the US Constitution, there are arguably constitutional limits to the government's intrusion into individuals' right to privacy even while carrying on a public purpose such as exercising police powers or passing legislation. The US Constitution, however, only protects against governments or government agencies, not, as in other countries such as Canada and the European Union, private companies. Invasions of privacy by individuals can only be remedied under common law.

The Fourth Amendment to the US Constitution ensures that "the right of the people to be secure in their persons, houses, papers, and effects, against unreasonable searches and seizures, shall not be violated, and no warrants shall issue, but upon probable cause, supported by oath or affirmation, and particularly describing the place to be searched, and the persons or things to be seized." These rights have been modified and have evolved over years of decisions by judges.

Unlike Canada, Australia, and the EU among others, the United States has avoided enacting general data protection rules in favor of specific "sectoral laws" governing specific industries or specific commercial sectors of the economy, rather than all businesses. For example, the Gramm-Leach-Bliley Act imposes restrictions on the ability of financial institutions to disclose nonpublic personal information about consumers to nonaffiliated third parties and requires financial institutions to provide privacy notices to consumers.

Other examples of sector specific laws include health privacy laws, online privacy laws, communication privacy laws, information privacy laws, and video rental records.

There is self-regulation, in which businesses and other entities voluntarily agree to keep information private, although there is no enforcement mechanism for a breach of this "self-regulation," and there is no individual right to appeal or right to compensation for privacy infringements.

One drawback with the sectoral approach to privacy used in the US is that it requires that new legislation be enacted each time a new technology is developed, therefore statutory protection can fall behind technology.

Although the European Commission has never issued a formal opinion on the adequacy of privacy protection in the US, "data exchange" between the US and Europe was questioned in the 1990s. Much of the data that crossed international borders is personal financial data about individuals. Europe had laws that safeguarded personal financial information. However, the Europeans thought US laws were lacking. The EU had concerns as to whether the United States' sectoral and self-regulatory approach to privacy protection would pass the "adequacy standards" of the EU laws on data privacy, thereby jeopardizing the continued flow of data between the EU and the US.

In 1998, the United States began negotiating a "Safe Harbor" agreement with the European Union in order to ensure the continued trans-border flows of personal data. The idea of the "Safe Harbor" was that United States companies would voluntarily self-certify to adhere to a set of privacy principles worked out by the United States Department of Commerce and the Internal Market Directorate of the European Commission. These companies would then have a presumption of adequacy and they could continue to receive personal data from countries in the European Union.

Clearly, people expect more privacy in their bedrooms and less at a Rolling Stones concert. Public figures and celebrities have to accept that their pictures will be taken. Private citizens may have more grounds to complain about their photo being taken because they have a reasonable expectation of privacy. The politician, rock star, and actor do not.

If the person was entitled to privacy, then the second question is whether the defendant (i.e., the person who is defending the claim and normally the one who either collected or used the private information or otherwise allegedly breached the plaintiff's privacy rights) actually breached the plaintiff's privacy. This analysis centers on the circumstances surrounding the invasion of privacy including any domestic or other relationship between the parties.

In British Columbia, Canada, the *Privacy Act* makes it a tort for one to, without authorization or consent, use the name, photograph, or portrait of another for the purpose of advertising, promoting the sale of, or trading in property or services. So unless I consent, you can't use that picture you took of me or the drawing you made of me to sell your toothpaste or your soap.

As with invasion of privacy, you can sue for "appropriation of personality" without having to prove you were damaged. The purpose of the tort of appropriation of personality is to protect the right of a person to not be an object of publicity without first giving consent. It also protects one's rights in the economic value of his or her personality or reputation. It is very similar to the concept of "passing off" found in Intellectual Property law. The right against passing off prevents a person from misrepresenting his or her goods or services as being the goods and services of another and prevents a person from presenting his or her goods or services as having some association or connection with another person when this is not true. The concern in intellectual property law and with appropriation of personality is that association with substandard goods or services may tarnish a person's reputation and this may have economic and/or social impacts.

Appropriation of personality is not a recognized tort in the United States. However, the US does have what is known as "personality rights" or "publicity rights," which is the right of an individual to control his or her own personality and publicity. Personality rights are property rights in the US and therefore a person may be capable of passing these rights to his or her heirs upon death. Each individual state creates its own laws regarding personality rights. There is no comprehensive federal regime.

1.2 The United States' approach to personal information

In the United States, jurisdiction over privacy and personal information protection issues is split between the State Legislatures and Federal Congress. There is no comprehensive federal legislation dealing with privacy and personal information issues in the private sector. Instead, each state enacts its own laws to deal with privacy and the collection, use, and disclosure of personal information. This means regulation is inconsistent from state to state and ultimately it falls to self-regulation.

The Federal Trade Commission (FTC) has taken on the role of protecting consumers' privacy. Under the FTC act, the FTC can enforce an organization's privacy policy in order to prevent unfairness and deception of consumers. For example, when the company Toysmart went into bankruptcy, it wanted to sell years of personal information of its customers collected through its website. This was in direct contradiction to its stated policy, which assured customers Toysmart would never share the personal information of its customers with a third party. The FTC stepped in to hold Toysmart to its privacy policy.

The FTC has powers granted under other laws and has implemented rules concerning financial privacy notices and the safeguarding of personal information. The FTC is particularly interested in protecting children and, due to the FTC's advocacy, the US Congress enacted the Children's Online Privacy Protection Act (COPPA). COPPA applies to operators of websites directed at, having a general audience of, or knowingly collecting information from children who are 13 years or younger. These operators must obtain verifiable parental consent *before* collecting personal information from children. This means the operator cannot collect information about the child unless parental consent is given.

1.3 Personal information in Canada

In Canada, the federal *Personal Information Protection and Electronic Documents Act* (PIPEDA) sets out legal rules for how private sector organizations like businesses may collect, use, or disclose one's personal information if they are collecting, using, or disclosing it in the course of their commercial activities. The law gives individuals the right to access and request correction of the personal information businesses may have collected about them.

PIPEDA applies to personal information collected, used, or disclosed by the retail sector, publishing companies, the service industry, manufacturers, and other provincially regulated organizations. British Columbia, Alberta, and Quebec are the only provinces with laws recognized as substantially similar to PIPEDA, and those provincial personal information laws apply in those provinces. Whether at the provincial or federal level, these laws regulate the collection, use, and disclosure of personal information by businesses and other organizations and provide individuals with a general right of access to, and correction of, their personal information. Ontario, although under PIPEDA, has adopted specific privacy legislation to protect personal health information.

Federal and provincial legislation in this area requires private-sector organizations to collect, use, or disclose one's personal information by fair and lawful means, with consent, and only for purposes that are reasonable. Private-sector organizations are also obliged to protect personal information through appropriate security measures, and to destroy it when it's no longer needed for the original purposes. Individuals have the right to expect the personal information the business maintains about them is accurate, complete, and up-to-date. That means individuals have a right to see personal information retained by the business, and to ask for corrections if the business has made a mistake.

If a business is not responding to an individual's complaint about how his or her personal information has been held or used, a complaint can be made with the federal or provincial privacy commissioner.

Generally, under Canadian federal and provincial legislation, before collecting, using, and/or disclosing personal information, a business or an organization must notify the person of the intended purpose and provide the opportunity for the person to consent or refuse consent. Personal information is information about an identifiable individual. This includes personal information about employees, but does not include employee contact or work product information. In other words, if your name and phone number are in the phone book, or you've given out a business card with your cell number, or your email address is in a directory of medical or legal professionals, that's "contact" information and not "personal" information. The business or organization can only collect personal information to the extent it needs in order to fulfill the stated purpose of collecting it. This is why you'll often see a privacy statement on a form you're filling out or a business's privacy policy on a web page you're accessing. The business has a legal obligation to notify you about what it is doing with the information it collects. (If you don't consent, you can always walk away from the transaction).

The purpose of both the federal and provincial laws is to balance a person's right to privacy and his or her desire to protect his or her personal information with the needs of organizations to collect, use, or disclose information for reasonable, appropriate, and lawful purposes.

The British Columbia *Personal Information Protection Act* (PIPA), like other privacy statutes in Canada, sets out requirements for how businesses and other organizations may collect, use, disclose, and secure one's personal information. Under PIPA, an individual has the right to —

- know why an organization collects, uses, or discloses personal information;

- expect an organization to collect, use, or disclose personal information reasonably and appropriately;

- be told who is responsible within an organization for protecting personal information;

- expect an organization to protect personal information by taking appropriate security measures;

- expect that the personal information used or disclosed by a business or organization is accurate and complete;

- request corrections to errors about personal information;

- request access to his or her personal information maintained with that business or organization;

- complain to the business or organization about how it collects, uses, or discloses personal information; and

- appeal if a dispute about personal information can't be resolved.

1.4 The United Kingdom's approach to personal information

The United Kingdom's approach to personal information is similar to Canada's. The UK enacted the *Data Protection Act* (DPA) that governs the processing of data about a "data subject," where processing means obtaining, recording, holding, organizing, adapting, altering, retrieving, consulting, using, disclosing, combining, erasing, or carrying out any operation on the data. The DPA also explicitly sets out a list of "sensitive personal data," which includes race, ethnic origin, political opinions, religious or other beliefs, membership in a trade union, physical or mental health, sexual life, and the commission or alleged commission of an offence and any proceedings for an offence.

The UK, similarly, has set out a number of exceptions and rights. One notable exception is for the collection, use, or disclosure of personal information for journalistic, artistic, and literary purposes.

With respect to rights, there are eight principles that reflect similar principles contained in Canada's laws. Specifically, in the UK, a person has the right to have his or her data processed fairly and lawfully according to his or her rights under the law. An organization may only collect data for specified and lawful purposes and cannot collect excessive data in relation to the purposes for collection. Data must be accurate, current, and not kept for any longer than is necessary. Organizations must ensure that measures are in place to protect against unlawful processing or accidental loss or destruction of personal data.

The UK does depart from Canada's approach with its final principle that personal data must not be transferred to a country or territory outside the European Union unless that country has an adequate level of protection for the rights and freedoms of data subjects.

2. Canada versus Facebook

Canada's Privacy Commissioner, Jennifer Stoddart, has been extremely active in pressuring Facebook and other social networking sites to change their privacy policies in Canada, which means changing their privacy policies throughout the world.

Facebook's founder, Mark Zuckerberg, had been widely quoted as saying that the social norms around privacy had evolved to the point where people had become very comfortable about sharing lots of information with more and more people and that "privacy is dead."

However, Stoddart's comments about social networking, privacy, and reputation are notable.

"It's no longer good enough to presume that if people 'click here' to say they've read the privacy policy, then their privacy concerns have been addressed. Even young, socially networked people continue to care about privacy … they just overestimate the privacy protections that exist in the online environment."

Canada's Privacy Commissioner performed a review of Facebook's privacy policies in 2009 arising from a complaint by the Canadian Internet Policy and Public Interest Clinic (CIPPIC). The investigation, which was described by Professor Dr. Michael Geist, of the University of Ottawa as "the most exhaustive official investigation of Facebook privacy practices anywhere in the world," found four main areas of concern, which Facebook responded to:

Third-party application developers: The sharing of personal information with more than one million third-party developers around the globe who were creating Facebook applications (e.g., games, quizzes) created serious privacy risks, and allowed those third-party developers to access users' personal information, and information about their online "friends." Facebook agreed in 2009 to retrofit its application platform so that applications will be prevented from accessing information until express consent is obtained for each category of personal information the application seeks to access. Users adding an application would be advised that the application seeks access to specific categories of personal information, so the users can control which categories of information an application is permitted to access.

Deactivation of account: Facebook provided confusing information about the distinction between account deactivation (personal information is held in digital storage) and deletion (personal information is actually erased from Facebook servers). As well, Facebook had not implemented a retention policy under which the personal information of users who have deactivated their accounts would be deleted from the site's servers after a reasonable length of time. Theoretically, Facebook could keep everything on its servers forever. Facebook agreed to make it clear to users that they have the option of either *deactivating* their account or *deleting* their account.

Personal information of non-users: The Privacy Commissioner stated that Facebook wasn't sufficiently protecting the privacy of non-users who were invited to join Facebook by users. Facebook agreed to include more information in its terms of use statement. Facebook maintained that it did not use email addresses to track the success of its invitation feature, nor did it maintain a separate email address list for this purpose.

Accounts of deceased users: The Privacy Commissioner stated that people should have a better way to provide meaningful consent to have their account memorialized after their death. As such, Facebook should be clear in its privacy policy that it will keep a user's profile online after death so that friends can post comments and pay tribute. Facebook agreed to change the wording in its privacy policy to explain what will happen in the event of a user's death.

Stoddart said in a speech made in April 2010, "Facebook, Street View and What's Next: Navigating Your Way Through New Issues in Privacy Law," that Facebook "eventually committed to a number of changes that would bring their social networking site in line with Canadian privacy law."

"They're not there yet and, in fact, we wound up launching another investigation in January [2010], in response to other changes they made to their privacy settings last December."

"But we are continuing to talk to them and to monitor their progress."

"Bear in mind that Facebook is a multinational giant with all the legal and technical backing necessary to know, understand, and respect the privacy laws of the countries in which they operate."

"It doesn't matter whether a company is Canadian or based elsewhere, virtual or real. It can be a new wireless firm in Toronto or a bank in an online community run out of Singapore. If it has an operating presence inside Canada, and is collecting the personal information of Canadians, then it is subject to Canadian law. There is no ambiguity about that."

"We expect organizations to know the law, and to understand and meet their responsibilities under it. We expect them to develop and implement privacy-enhancing innovations, and to communicate with their customers about privacy."

3. Defamation

If you're blogging, writing commentary for print or online publications or message boards, or even if you're regularly posting status updates to Facebook, and your comments are edgy in that you're critical of people or companies, you ought to have a basic understanding of the law of defamation.

A person or a company has a right to their good reputation and the law of defamation is the legal way in which people protect and vindicate their good reputations. A statement will be defamatory in Canada if it is one that tends to discredit or lower an individual's reputation "in the estimation of right-thinking members of society generally" or otherwise exposes the defamed person to hatred, contempt, or ridicule, or injures his or her reputation in an office, trade, or profession.

The law of defamation doesn't try to protect you from a personal insult or a comment that simply hurts your feelings or injures your pride. It's meant to protect your reputation in the community, not your feelings. For example, if someone says you're overweight, you have bad breath, or you're not very pretty, you might have hurt feelings, but not much of a legal case. However, if you're accused of stealing from the charity you raise money for, or being crooked in business, and this comment is made to another or recorded in some permanent form, you may well have a claim.

Defamatory words or actions may affect people in different ways, such as affecting their social reputation resulting in a loss of friends, or affecting their business reputation resulting in a loss of business or loss of an opportunity for economic gain. People and corporations may be defamed and may sue for defamation if their reputations have been impugned. The words may be spoken or written, sometimes expressed as libel and slander. A defamatory statement that is spoken without permanence is slander. A defamatory statement that is communicated in writing or some other permanent media such as a newspaper article, a magazine article, on television, or on radio, and for our purposes, by way of email transmissions, message boards, blogs, chat rooms, YouTube, texts, or Facebook posts is called libel.

Although the distinction between libel and slander isn't as important as it was 200 years ago (lawyers normally combine the two concepts under the umbrella of defamation), there is one important difference. If a statement is slanderous (e.g., I slander you by making an untrue oral comment about you that tarnishes your reputation), then you as the plaintiff must prove actual harm to your reputation in order to recover damages. You have to prove that what I said harmed you.

When libel is alleged (e.g., I made a defamatory statement about you in a newspaper article, a magazine article, on television, on radio, by email, on a message board, on a blog, in a chat room, in a text, on a Facebook post, or on YouTube), harm to your reputation is assumed and a court will award damages without actual proof of harm.

Damages can be higher if your "standing in the community" is higher, whether because you are in politics, business, church or charitable activities, or otherwise. In such cases, your reputation is arguably "worth more" and a defamer will have to pay higher damages for besmirching your good name. Be assured if comments are made via email or in blogs, message boards, forums, and on Facebook, they have the potential to be defamatory and legally actionable if they harm a person's reputation.

To succeed in a defamation action in Canada, first a plaintiff must prove that the material communicated was defamatory (in the sense that it discredited or lowered an individual's reputation in society or otherwise exposed the plaintiff to hatred, contempt, or ridicule, or injured his or her reputation in an office, trade, or profession). Second, the statement must refer to the plaintiff. Third, the statement must have been communicated to another person or persons. Whether the defamer had intention to defame is not relevant to whether there is defamation, as intent is not relevant.

A defamatory statement made online is arguably more serious, given the extensive use of the Internet by way of blogs, email, forums, message boards, and comments made through online social networks.

The harm that can be done is arguably more serious than defamatory statements made in a local paper or on TV given the fact that anything on the Internet can be read or viewed by millions of people around the world many times, and those people can alert millions more to read or view the content.

Sometimes, it's the very intention of the defamer to reach a worldwide audience because the defamer believes he or she is fighting a "crusade" against a large corporation with greater financial, public relations, and communications resources; the Internet being the only way (and perhaps the least expensive way) to make his or her point, especially if the defamer presumes he or she will be anonymous. To the defamer, the Internet levels the playing field.

There are defenses to an action for defamation:

Truth: If a statement that's alleged to be defamatory is actually true, then that statement cannot have impugned or otherwise damaged a good reputation. Generally, a defamatory statement is not actionable if it can be proven to be true. Truth is the best defense, and it's consistent with the principle of free speech.

Consent: If the complainant actually agreed to the publication of defamatory statements, or that those statements were made at the complainant's request or encouragement, then a defendant won't be liable.

Privilege: In the interest of free speech and the free flow of communication and discourse, free speech is weighed against the right a person has to his or her good reputation. Defamatory statements made in court or parliament are privileged and, even if they are defamatory and false, there will be no liability.

However, there is also something called "qualified privilege" to make a defamatory statement in certain circumstances. For example, where an employer comments negatively about the performance of a former employee if he or she is asked to provide a reference by a potential new employer, as long as the opinion about the employee is not given in bad faith, it's normally privileged. As long as a critical comment about a former employee is given in good faith, and only made on a need-to-know basis (i.e., not widely circulated), the former employer's critical review that the employee's performance was poor, or he or she was "toxic" in the work environment, or took too many breaks, is protected by this qualified privilege. This is to ensure the free flow of sensitive information isn't biased by the fear of legal action for an employer's honest comment. Thus an unflattering restaurant review, or TripAdvisor comment, or comment on a message board about a bad product or service may fall into the category of qualified privilege, or truth.

Fair Comment is the defense that's used by the media generally when there is an allegation that a statement made in the media has defamed a person. Journalists who make a comment on matters of public interest have an immunity from liability, even where their comments are defamatory, as long as the comments were made in good faith and without malice, and the defamatory comments expressed an "honest opinion on facts that are true and known to persons to whom the comment is made."

The Supreme Court of Canada fundamentally changed the defense as a result of three decisions rendered in 2009 and 2010. Journalists and other publishers aren't just limited to the defense of "truth" or "qualified privilege" or "fair comment." Now added is the defense of "responsible communication in the public interest." Journalists are now protected from libel lawsuits even if the statements made by them were not true, as long as the news was urgent, serious, and of public importance, and the journalist used reliable sources, and tried to obtain and report the other side of the story. "Journalist" was not limited to mainstream media journalism, but now includes Internet bloggers and other creators and publishers of content that is in the public interest, whose opinions and reporting are only accessible on the Internet.

3.1 Anonymity doesn't exist online

Just because a comment is made anonymously or under a pseudonym in a blog, on an online forum, or on Facebook doesn't mean you're anonymous. And it doesn't mean that your speech might not be defamatory.

New York blogger Rosemary Port learned the hard way that anonymous blogs aren't anonymous anymore. Fashion model Liskula Cohen sued Google Inc. (on behalf of its subsidiary blogger.com) for the identity of the anonymous blogger of "Skanks in NYC," who Cohen argued, defamed her in online comments relating to Cohen's sexual proclivities and called her a "psychotic, lying, whoring … skank." Cohen couldn't sue the alleged defamer because the blog was anonymous. She could only sue the defamer if she knew his or her identity, so she sued to obtain the blogger's identity. The court agreed with Cohen and ordered Google to disclose the identity of Port.

Whether the comments were defamatory or not wasn't the issue. The issue was whether she could obtain the identities of potential defamers so she could consider suing them. Whether the comments were defamatory or not would be something left to another court.

Of note is that Port (whose name was released) is now suing Google for $15 million for releasing her identity. Said Port's lawyer in an interview, "I'm ready to take this all the way to the Supreme Court. Our Founding Fathers wrote 'The Federalist Papers' under pseudonyms. Inherent in the First Amendment is the right to speak anonymously. Shouldn't that right extend to the new public square of the Internet?"

Google spokesperson Andrew Pederson was quoted in *The New York Times* saying that Google "sympathize[s] with anyone who may be the victim of cyberbullying ... We also take great care to respect privacy concerns and will only provide information about a user in response to a subpoena or other court order. If content is found by a court to be defamatory, we will, of course, remove it immediately."

Another case was in Halifax, Nova Scotia, where the Supreme Court of Nova Scotia was asked by two of Halifax's senior fire fighters to disclose the names of people who posted anonymous comments on a newspaper's website that they say defamed them. The stories involved allegations of racism in the Halifax Fire Department against Chief Bill Mosher and Deputy Chief Stephen Thurber. They sought an order from the court, which required *The Coast* to identify seven people who posted comments on its online site between April, 2009 to March 20, 2010. That order was granted and the names of the people who posted the comments were disclosed.

Keith Pridgen, a student at the University of Calgary, posted on a Facebook group called "I no longer fear hell, I took a course from [name of instructor]." His post criticized his former law professor. Pridgen posted "[name of instructor] is no longer teaching any courses at the U of C. Remember when she told us she was a long-term prof? Well actually she was only a sessional and picked up our class at the last moment because another prof wasn't able to do it ... lucky us. Well anyways I think we should all congratulate ourselves for leaving a [instructor's name]-free legacy for future students."

The University of Calgary determined that some of the comments were defamatory and Pridgen was placed on academic probation for six months owing to nonacademic misconduct. The instructor was not hired back for another semester. Pridgen applied for judicial review and challenged the University's decision on the basis of freedom of speech and his fundamental right to make critical remarks.

According to Pridgen's lawyer, freedom of speech on Facebook "is a sacred right. A right which is granted by the [Canadian] constitution." The University's lawyers argued that some of the criticisms were defamatory and that it had authority for disciplining students criticizing the competency of its instructors on social media sites such as Facebook.

4. Lawyers May Gain Access to Your Facebook Account

In the case of *Leduc v. Roman*, Justice D. M. Brown of the Superior Court of Justice in Ontario allowed the defendant insurance company access to all the plaintiff's Facebook pages. The plaintiff had been in an accident but the insurer believed the plaintiff was exaggerating the injury and was engaging in physical activities inconsistent with the injury. Knowing he had a Facebook page, the insurance company wanted full access to all the pages, even though some pages were public and some were private.

The court said, "that a person's Facebook profile may contain documents relevant to the issues in a [legal] action is beyond controversy. Photographs of parties posted to their Facebook profiles have been admitted as evidence relevant to demonstrating a party's ability to engage in sports and other recreational activities where the plaintiff has put his enjoyment of life or ability to work in issue."

The issue in *Leduc v. Roman* was that some of the plaintiff's Facebook information was public and some of it was private and therefore available only to "friends." Although there is law that a party to litigation can't go on a "fishing expedition" looking for information, the court concluded that there was likely to be relevant photographs relating to the accident or the plaintiff's physical condition on the private Facebook pages. The court determined that Facebook was a social networking site where, by definition, people posted photographs of themselves in various activities. Chances were that if the plaintiff's public site contained photographs that were relevant to the accident and his injuries, his private site would as well. The Judge discounted any significant privacy concerns:

"Having considered these competing interests, I have concluded that any invasion of privacy is minimal and is outweighed by the defendant's need to have the photographs in order to assess the case. The plaintiff could not have a serious expectation of privacy given that 366 people have been granted access to the private site 'as friends.'" Accordingly, the Judge ordered the plaintiff to produce copies of the webpage postings of his private Facebook pages. The Judge said:

"Where a party makes extensive postings of personal information on his or her publicly accessible Facebook profile, few production issues arise. Any relevant public postings by a party are producible [in this country]. Where in addition to a publicly accessible profile a party maintains a private Facebook profile viewable only by the party's 'friend' … it is reasonable to infer from the presence of content on the party's public profile that similar content likely exists on the private profile. A court can then order the production of relevant postings [and photographs] on the private profile. Facebook is not used as a means by which account holders carry on monologues with themselves; it is a device by which users share with others information about who they are, what they like, what they do, and where they go, in varying degrees of detail. Facebook profiles are not designed to function as diaries. [In this case] it is reasonable to infer that a social networking site likely contains some content relevant to the issue of how Mr. Leduc has been able to lead his life since the accident. However, the mere proof of the existence of a Facebook profile does not entitle a party to gain access to all the material placed on that site. Only material that relates to the matter in issue — a car accident and one's personal activities after the accident where the party's answers revealed that his Facebook profile contains content that may relate to issues in an action, production can be ordered of the relevant content."

Something else to consider when it comes to lawyers accessing information online is the "relationship status" feature on Facebook. If you are going through a divorce, instead of announcing it, you should probably stay off Facebook until the divorce is final. According to the Academy of Matrimonial Lawyers (AAML), "Facebook holds the distinction of being the unrivaled leader for online divorce evidence with 66 percent citing it as the primary source."

The president of AAML, Marlene Eskind Moses says, "Going through a divorce always results in heightened levels of personal scrutiny. If you publicly post any contradictions to previously made statements and promises, an estranged spouse will certainly be one of the first people to notice and make use of that evidence."

The lesson here is the more you share about yourself online, the more chance others have of using that information against you.

5. Social Media and the Central Intelligence Agency (CIA)

The Central Intelligence Agency (CIA) is investing in technology designed to better monitor Twitter, blogs, YouTube, and consumer buying habits on eBay, reading habits on Amazon, and a host of other information posted by individuals online. The fear is that terrorists would use the Internet to communicate with each other anonymously across borders.

The investment arm of the CIA, In-Q-Tel, has invested funds in a software company that monitors social media, that is, Visible Technologies. Noah Shachtman wrote "Exclusive: US Spies Buy Stake in Firm That Monitors Blogs, Tweets," (October 19, 2009) in *Wired* magazine, "It's part of a larger movement within the spy services to get better at using 'open source intelligence' — information that's publicly available, but often hidden in the flood of TV shows, newspaper articles, blog posts, online videos, and radio reports generated every day."

The article also notes that "Visible crawls over half a million web 2.0 sites a day, scraping more than a million posts and conversations taking place on blogs, online forums, Flickr, YouTube, Twitter, and Amazon. Customers get customized, real-time feeds of what's being said on these sites, based on a series of keywords."

7
TEENAGERS SEXTING, CYBERBULLYING, AND ACADEMIC DISHONESTY

One of the more troublesome and disconcerting aspects of online communication is communication by children and teens on cell phones, and other mobile devices that allow for the transmission of text and images from device to device, or from the device to the Internet, outside any supervision by parents or other adults. This chapter will look at the problem of sexting by teens specifically, cyberbullying, and academic dishonesty.

1. Sexting

Cell phone use among adults is staggering in the industrialized world, but perhaps the use of cell phones by teens is just as endemic.

According to the Pew Research Center, in 2004, 18 percent of 12-year-olds in the United States owned (or had regular use of) cell phones. In 2009, 58 percent of 12-year-olds owned (or had regular use of) cell phones. Also in 2009, 83 percent of 17-year-olds owned (or had regular use of) a cell phone. Many of these teens used their cell phones for a number of purposes in addition to merely phoning another person. One of the more disturbing consequences of easy online digital communications over mobile devices such as cell phones is so-called "sexting," which is a word combination of "sex" and "texting."

A survey performed in 2009 conducted by Pew Internet & American Life Project, conducted telephone surveys of teens aged 12 to 18 about their cell phone use and particularly, whether they had ever sent out or received sexually suggestive nude or nearly nude photos or videos of themselves or of someone they knew, on their cell phones.

Interestingly enough, the study intentionally stayed away from studying the transmission of sexually suggestive text messages without images. Some definitions of sexting include "sexually suggestive text," but the Pew study was only interested in the transmission of sexual images, perhaps because the transmission of sexual images might have criminal law implications where the transmission of text would not. Nor did the Pew study examine sexual images transmitted through other means such as through email or through other social networks.

What Pew really wanted to study was the recording of a nude or nearly nude photo or video on cameras in cell phones, and the transmission of those images to someone else with a cell phone.

In addition to the telephone survey Pew conducted in October 2009, Pew, in conjunction with the University of Michigan, also created focus groups with teens aged 12 to 18. Certain teens within those focus groups took part in a private survey in which they wrote about their experiences with sexting.

Amanda Lenhart, Senior Research Specialist and author of "Teens and Sexting" (the Pew study) discussed what the teens said to the researchers: "Teens explained to us how sexually suggestive images have become a form of relationship currency," she said in the report. "These images are shared as a part of or instead of sexual activity, or as a way of starting or maintaining a relationship with a significant other. And they are also passed along to friends for their entertainment value, as a joke or for fun."

Teens also described to researchers within the focus groups the pressure they are under to share these nude or nearly nude digital images. One high school girl wrote as part of her contribution to the study: "When I was about 14–15 years old, I received/sent these types of pictures. Boys usually ask for them or start that type of conversation. My boyfriend, or someone I really liked asked for them. And I felt like if I didn't do it, they wouldn't continue to talk to me. At the time, it was no big deal. But now looking back it was definitely inappropriate and over the line."

The Pew study found the following other information about sexting:

- 75 percent of all teens surveyed owned or had regular use of a cell phone and 66 percent of those teens used their cell phones for text messaging.

- 4 percent of cell phone owning teens aged 12 to 17 said in the survey that they had sent sexually suggestive nude or nearly nude images of themselves to someone else via text messaging.

- 15 percent of cell phone owning teens aged 12 to 17 said that they had received sexually suggestive nude or nearly nude images of someone they knew on their cell phones.

- Older teens were much more likely to send and receive nude or nearly nude images. Indeed, 8 percent of 17-year-olds with cell phones acknowledged that they had sent sexually provocative images by text, and 30 percent of 17-year-olds acknowledged they had received nude or nearly nude images on their cell phone.

- Interestingly enough, teens who paid for their own cell phone bills were more likely to send "sext" messages than teens who did not directly pay their cell bills. The study revealed that 17 percent of teens who paid for all of the costs associated with their own cell phones sent sexually suggestive images by text. But only 3 percent of teens who did not pay for, or only paid for a portion of cell phone costs sent sexual images, suggesting that when parents have a part to play in the payment of their children's cell phone bills (presumably because they are monitoring, and questioning the costs of these bills), they are more inclined to discover this kind of behavior and deal with it.

- Focus groups surveyed by Pew and by the University of Michigan concluded that there were three main scenarios for sexting: First, an exchange of images solely between two romantic partners. Second, exchanges between partners that are shared with others outside the relationship. Third, exchanges between teens who are not yet in a relationship but where at least one person hopes to be.

- Teens who are more intense users of cell phones are more likely to receive sexually suggestive images. For these teens, the cell phone has become such an important vehicle and conduit for communication and content of all kinds that "turning it off is nearly unthinkable."

Said Lenhart, "The desire for risk-taking and sexual exploration during the teenage years combined with a constant connection via mobile devices creates a 'perfect storm' for sexting. Teenagers have always grappled with issues around sex and relationships, but their coming-of-age mistakes and transgressions have never been so easily transmitted and archived for others to see."

1.1 Serious legal and social consequences

A 15-year-old girl is interested in a 17-year-old boy in high school. The boy is about to turn 18 and become a legal adult, and graduate, with his eyes on college. She takes a partially nude photo of herself with her cell phone and sends it to him. Maybe she wants to appear sexy or willing or provocative and interesting. Maybe she just wants him to like her. He receives the picture, and at some point, he forwards the sext message to a friend, who forwards it to someone else in his school. It makes the rounds at school and gets into the hands of the girl's parents, who contact the police. The boy turns 18 just before charges are laid for possession of and distribution of child pornography.

This isn't a law school exam filled with hypothetical issues to spot and opine on for the professor. These issues are happening today. In the United States, these sexting issues are occurring regularly. On the one hand, it's a battle between those who see sexting in the same vein as underage drinking, teenage sex, and other rites of passage that should be dealt with as a social issue rather than a criminal one. On the other hand, there are the politicians, religious leaders, and prosecutors who seek to use the full weight of the criminal law to punish those who would take, send, receive, and retransmit nude images from cell phone to cell phone.

George Skumanick, Jr., a Pennsylvania district attorney, threatened a number of students with possession and distribution of child pornography after a sexting incident at a high school. The issue arose when a student's cell phone was confiscated in class, and her teacher discovered nude images that had been sexted to other high school students in the same school.

The district attorney demanded that the students (there were close to 20 involved at one point) take a five-week counseling program plus probation, or he would press child pornography charges. "An adult would go to prison for this," he said in an interview with CNN. com. "If you take the photo, you've committed a crime. If you send the photo, you've committed a different crime, but it's essentially the same crime."

The parents of some of the girls who were implicated launched a legal action against the district attorney with the assistance of the American Civil Liberties Union. One argument involved unreasonable search and seizure (i.e., the teacher that seized the cell phone in class had no legal right to take away and inspect the contents of the cell phone). Another argument was that the images could not constitute pornography and the girls in question could not be charged with distribution of Internet pornography if the girls did not consent to the distribution of the images pictured.

In an article for CNN.com International, authors Deborah Feyerick and Sheila Steffen wrote about the plight of 18-year-old Phillip Alpert, who is listed as a registered sex offender for the next 25 years in Florida because he was convicted of sending nude images of his then 16-year-old girlfriend to her family and friends after a breakup with her, as revenge.

"It was a stupid thing I did," Alpert told Feyerick and Steffen for the article. "Because I was upset and tired and it was the middle of the night and I was an immature kid. You will find me on the registered sex offender list next to people who have raped children … "

Alpert's lawyer, Larry Walters, is trying to get Alpert's name removed from the sex offender registry. Walters told CNN.com that the law lags behind the technology, "Sexting is treated as child pornography in almost every state and it catches teens completely off guard because this is a fairly natural and normal thing for them to do. It is surprising to us as parents, but for teens it's part of their culture." He also added, "Some judges have the good sense and reasonableness to treat this as a social problem and others are more zealous in their efforts to put everybody away and I think it's time as a society that we step back a little bit and avoid this temptation to lock up our children."

Alpert can't get a passport to travel outside the United States, and is having trouble finding employment. "I'm being punished for the rest of my life for something that took two minutes or less to do."

In the United States, 38 states include juvenile sex offenders in their sex offender registries. Other US states will register juveniles as sex offenders if they are tried as adults, or if they are older than 14, or in some states, 15. Most US states allow anyone with an Internet connection to be able to find people listed on sex offender registries.

Another example is 18-year-old Jesse Logan who sent a nude photo of herself to a boy she was dating. She later learned that the photo circulated among students at area high schools, and she had to endure harassment and cyberbullying about the photo and her reputation from other girls in her school; the quintessential "mean girls" of her school. School officials apparently didn't help or didn't want to get involved, because the activity didn't involve school and hadn't taken place at the school. Logan even gave a television interview in the hope that this would stop the bullying and harassment, but it didn't. Logan committed suicide. Her parents now warn others about the problems with sexting and are campaigning to have the laws changed to deal with it. At the time of writing, the boy who circulated the sext to his friends was not charged with anything.

In September, 2010, Canadians were shocked by the report of an alleged vicious sexual assault by seven boys on a 16-year-old girl who was allegedly drugged and gang raped after a rave party near Pitt Meadows, British Columbia. At the time of writing, police had arrested two suspects and were obtaining evidence to lay charges on others.

As repugnant as the event was, one of the observers took photos of the gang rape as it happened, and posted the photos to Facebook. When advised, Facebook immediately removed the photographs from the site, but not before copies had been saved to individual hard drives on other computers and recirculated. The photographs went viral within days.

The 16-year-old boy who took the photographs and uploaded them to Facebook was arrested by police, and prosecutors have charged the youth with producing and distributing child pornography.

2. Cyberbullying

Cyberbullying is term that was unheard of a decade ago. The definition of cyberbullying is, "willful and repeated harm inflicted through the use of computers, cell phones, and other electronic devices."

The Cyberbullying Research Center states that one in five middle school students in the US has been the victim of some kind of Cyberbullying (i.e., a threat sent by email or text on a cell phone or through an online social network).

In an article in *The New York Times*, June 27, 2010, reporter Jan Hoffman wrote that "Online Bullies Pull Schools into the Fray." The story discussed a 12-year-old girl who was receiving threatening text messages from a 12-year-old boy at her school. The parents went to the school's principal, who decided the school couldn't do anything about it.

"This occurred out of school, on a weekend," the school's principal, Tony Orsini said. "We can't discipline him."

Sometimes an appropriate response by school officials is one of the more perplexing issues in cyberbullying, as school officials are reluctant to get involved when the activity occurs outside of the school and not during school hours.

In another study conducted by Pew Internet & American Life Project ("Cyberbullying and Online Teens," June 27, 2007), researchers surveyed 935 Internet-using teenagers by telephone. The survey revealed that one third (32 percent) of all teenagers who used the Internet and were part of the study admit they had been targets of "annoying and potentially menacing online activities," which included receiving threatening messages; having their private emails or text messages forwarded without consent to others; having embarrassing pictures of them distributed or posted to an online social network without permission; or having rumors about them spread online. The Pew report concluded that cyberbullying may be annoying or relatively benign or may be truly threatening.

The study also concluded that girls were more likely than boys to be targets of cyberbullying; and teens who share their identities and thoughts online through social networks such as Facebook and MySpace were more likely to be targets than are those who led less active lives online.

The study concluded with this dire warning "Bullying has entered the digital age. The impulses behind it are the same, but the effect is magnified. In the past, the materials of bullying would have been whispered, shouted, or passed around. Now, with a few clicks, a photo, video, or a conversation can be shared with hundreds via email or millions through a website, online profile, or blog posting."

Samantha Wilson, a former police officer and internationally recognized expert in child and family safety is the founder of the child safety organization called Kidproof, which offers courses and training to raise child-safety awareness by empowering children and parents with knowledge that they can draw from in case of an emergency or dangerous situation. She is also the author of *Safe Kids, Safe Families* (HarperCollins, 2005).

Wilson says, "Kids do not have the same filters and critical thinking skills that adults have, and often make choices based on the 'now' and have no consideration for future consequences. Unfortunately, images that were originally sent as a joke or for private communication can easily become public and permanent."

Wilson also says, "We are hearing more and more cases of 'sextortion,' where an online predator finds sexual images sent through the Internet, and uses the threat to extort the victim into providing more images for his or her use. Kids caught in a sextortion scam are unlikely to report it for fear of discipline, embarrassment, and retribution, and therefore, usually comply with the predator's demands."

She says parents can protect their kids from sexting or becoming victims of sextortion or cyberbullying by following these tips:

- Keep the lines of communication open at all times. Be sure that your kids know that they can come to you for any reason without fear of rejection or judgment.

- Talk to them early. Don't wait until they are teenagers to have an Internet-safety discussion. The fastest growing group of Internet users are preschool age.

- Seek help. If your child finds he or she is in a potentially risky situation, or you believe that the child is being cyberbullied, harassed, or even involved in sextortion, report it to the police.

- Establish clear guidelines for the use of technology and devices. Right and wrong are the same online as they are in person. Have clear consequences for broken rules.

- Learn the technology for yourself. You cannot protect your children from something that you don't understand.

Wilson is also concerned about the next wave in online sexual communication, fuelled by the video functions of iPhones, new generation iPods, and other mobile devices with video capability. She says, "Instead of sending still sexual images, kids are now able to send *live* sexual images through these devices and 'sexviding' is considered to be 'the next thing' to sexting. The same problems that exist regarding still images exist for sexviding, but it's far, far worse, in that the iPhone, new generation iPod, and other similar devices work through Wi-Fi and not a more secure phone line. This makes it even easier for a hacker to intercept and convert the videos to his or her own use."

3. Academic Dishonesty

Cheating in high school, college, or university is a very serious matter and can result in failing the course in question, suspension, or even expulsion, adversely affecting the student's ability to graduate and perhaps even get employed after graduation. It's a career limiting move that can ruin a reputation, and the online world has made it far easier to cheat in school, college, or university, making the job of the teacher, instructor, or professor all the more challenging. Students don't hide a formula on the inside of their hat anymore. They use the Internet, Facebook, or smartphones.

A recent report by the Canadian Council on Learning (CCL) titled "Liars, Fraudsters and Cheats: Dealing with the growth of academic dishonesty" indicates that cheating is rampant, and a combination of the Internet and smartphones has made it easier to do and harder to catch. Close to 20,000 students from 11 post-secondary institutions were surveyed as part of the study. For the study, first-year university students were surveyed about their experience in high school. Of those students, 73 percent admitted to at least one instance of "serious cheating" on written work performed in high school. The study defined "serious cheating on written work" as —

- copying material from a written source or from the Internet without adequate paraphrasing or without acknowledging the source;

- turning in work done by someone else or copying and turning in large sections of another's work; and

- fabricating or falsifying a bibliography or data, or turning in a paper obtained from a "paper mill." (**Note:** A paper mill is an essay-writing company that create papers for students to hand in as their own work.)

The study reported that at the University of Waterloo, occurrences of cheating and plagiarism rose by 81 per cent between 2003 and 2006, and reported cases of online and Internet-based plagiarism tripled. Not surprisingly, the Internet is blamed for this trend towards academic dishonesty.

Students cut and paste directly from online sources into their own essays without references or sources and try to pass the work off as their own. Or they'll use a pay-for service such as an essay-writing company (i.e., paper mill) that creates papers for students to hand in as their own work.

The study states that the majority of students today are "digital natives," and have essentially grown up using computers, cell phones, and other devices, so they're comfortable with technology. However, "technological literacy" as the study calls it, seems to help some students try to engage in certain forms of academic dishonesty.

High-speed Internet access allows students to find and retrieve information easily and quickly from Wikipedia, or other online sources, and the study reveals that the chances of getting caught are often low. Cited in the study were a number of recent US surveys and studies, including one by Common Sense Media ("Hi-Tech Cheating: Cell Phones and Cheating in Schools, A National Poll"). It revealed that 52 percent of US students in Grade 7 through Grade 12 who were part of the survey admitted to some form of Internet-enabled cheating. Of the respondents, 38 percent had "cut and pasted" material from websites and submitted it as their own work, 32 percent had searched the Internet for course manuals designed for teachers to find the answers to the questions or problems posed in the student's textbooks, and 21 percent had downloaded papers from the Internet and submitted them as their own work.

Another study referred to in the CCL report found that 35 percent of high school students admitted to cheating at least once with a cell phone; 26 percent of this group had stored notes on their cell phones to review during their exams; 25 percent had texted friends for answers; 20 percent had searched the Internet for answers; and 17 percent had actually taken photographs of exam questions and transmitted them to others via their cell phones.

The study concluded that BlackBerrys and other smartphones make cheating easier. It also said that Internet-based cheating is difficult to monitor and might make it tempting for people to cheat.

3.1 How to prevent academic dishonesty

There are technologies that can assist teachers, professors, and other learning professionals with online cheating. Although one might copy a "suspect phrase" from the essay and look for uses of that phrase on Google, or get suspicious because the fonts in the essay differ from page to page, this is a "hit or miss strategy" and the "evidence" might be circumstantial and explainable (e.g., "I changed fonts halfway through the essay and forgot to change the whole paper").

This has led to the establishment of businesses that have developed more reliable technologies to spot plagiarists and copiers. One of them is Turnitin, which is the brand name for a software program that will use its database and algorithms to identify essays that may have been plagiarized. Other companies offer similar services to those of Turnitin; for example, CheckForPlagiarism.net, Copyscape, and EVE2.

Essentially though, all these services search the Web for similar phraseology using sophisticated algorithms. The mere checking of a paper for plagiarism using some of these services uploads the student's paper into a database so that other papers in the future will be compared with it.

Turnitin's website indicates that the company "got its start in 1996, when a group of researchers at UC Berkeley created a series of computer programs to monitor the recycling of research papers in their large undergraduate classes." Turnitin has access to a database of millions of paper-mill papers, previously submitted papers, articles, newspapers, and journals online. It uses a webcrawler to continuously monitor and update information. The program runs algorithms that are designed to catch similar phraseology, words, word order, diction, syntax, and other similar features to what is available on the database. The parent corporation of Turnitin, iParadigms, also sells other plagiarism detection services for newspapers, and book and magazine publishers called iThenticate.

Turnitin indicates that students will also use creative tricks to defeat anti-plagiarism software programs. For example, students might use an "e" from a different alphabet, such as Cyrillic, which is hardly noticeable to readers, but might well defeat software programs looking for the "e" in our alphabet. Euro signs for "e," or dollar signs for "s," or even "white text" to create spaces between words (where the spaces between words are actually letters in white text to confuse software that is looking for exact words and syntax) are the sorts of things that have been tried. Spammers use similar strategies to avoid their spam messages being caught by spam filters. Turnitin's algorithms catch these tricks.

The company admits that it doesn't find plagiarism but, rather, generates a "similarity index," which indicates that a student's text matches something in the Turnitin databases. Teachers might confront a student with this information, and seek an explanation, or use it as a tool to show how to avoid plagiarism in the future. Institutions using Turnitin require students to keep their papers in the database to protect their work from future plagiarism by others and perhaps as a teaching tool. This, however, may be a means of dealing with arguments made by students that this kind of software presumes students are guilty. It won't prevent well-off students from paying someone smarter to write original, custom papers that aren't in Turnitin's database before it's delivered to the student who bought it.

EssayPlant.com is a company that does just that in an effort to avoid Turnitin's database and algorithms:

"Do you urgently need a Custom Written Essay, Term Paper or a Research Paper? Do you stay up all night because the deadline for your essay is tomorrow? Do you feel helpless when you get a big homework assignment for your business class and you still have not written anything for sociology, literature, philosophy or other classes? EssayPlant offers you a highly competitive Custom Writing Solution!"

"At EssayPlant we know your essay writing needs because we hire college and university graduates and professors to provide the Best Custom Writing Service on the market and to free some of your time for individual studying. We write on virtually every topic and meet every deadline! We know what is required in your university and can provide you with the right Custom Essay, Term Paper, Book Report, or Research Paper just in time! All papers written by EssayPlant are authentic — we build knowledge from scratch!"

Perhaps educators will deal with this in the future by relying on more heavily weighted written and oral examinations for a student's grades, or by returning to handwritten essays.

See Chapter 8 for information on metadata in Word documents.

8
THE DANGERS
OF METADATA

Let's turn to the issue of "metadata" in digital images and, more importantly, in MS Word and other word processing documents. What's metadata? It's a Greek word, and it means "data about data." If the online world is a binary world of zeros and ones, then the concept of data about data is important. It's the information behind the images and the words, like layers of an onion, or an iceberg below the waterline. Metadata is also information about the history, tracking, or management of an electronic image or document. Failure to appreciate its importance could be career limiting.

1. Digital Images

Let's look at the data behind data in digital images. If someone has recently sent you a digital photograph by email, and you save it by dragging it to your desktop, you can easily find information such as the size of the photo, resolution of the image, and the date it was taken just by hitting "Control >Get Info" in Mac, and "Properties" in Windows.

I just opened an email from a friend of mine containing some boating photographs which he took a few summers ago. Using the Control >Get Info function in Mac, I can see that the photo is a 96 kb JPEG and was taken with a Panasonic DMC-FZ7 Camera at 1/500 of a second on August 2, 2008. Even though I've now deleted the email the photo was attached to and emptied my trash, the photograph is still saved on my computer along with its metadata. Like fingerprints, DNA, and footprints at a crime scene, the metadata shows my friend's email address!

Do this yourself the next time someone sends you a photograph by email. There is always more to a digital image than the image itself. Remember when you're sending digital photographs by email, the metadata not only contains data about the photograph (i.e., camera, exposure, date), but can include data about the photographer and sender of the email that contained the photograph.

If an image is pulled from the web, it can often retain its meta-data. For example, I just pulled a picture of a portrait of William Shakespeare from the Web. I can't recall where I pulled it from, but I was in Google looking for "Shakespeare image," found one I liked, and dragged it to my desktop.

Using Control>Get info on my Mac, I see that the image is a JPEG with a size of 100kb, saved to my desktop April 12, 2010. Its size is 300 x 389 and my own computer tells me where the image is from. Pull any digital image to your desktop from the online version of a newspaper or magazine and you'll find, using the same functions described above, that the metadata behind the image is still part of the image.

Note that metadata can be changed. I write a regular column for *The Globe and Mail*, and for each column, they use a photograph of me that was professionally taken by a Vancouver photographer. I dragged my own picture from one of my columns to my desktop to see the metadata behind my own photo. It thankfully doesn't indicate the original photographer or my email address (I emailed it to them, after all) but I see that my own image is identified as http://beta.images.theglobeandmail.com/archive/00385/Tony_Wilson_385207gm-c.jpeg. This means that whatever metadata was on the photo I sent to *The Globe and Mail* has been scrubbed and replaced by new meta-data. What happened to the metadata attached to the photograph of me? It was "scrubbed" of its metadata by software used by *The Globe and Mail*. Although one might try to adjust the photograph's embedded information in Properties (in Windows) and in Control >Get Info in Mac, I found I couldn't adjust or remove the metadata, indicating to me at least, that unless you're professionally trained in the operating systems of Windows or Mac, you really ought to acquire and use software specifically created to scrub all digital information from photographs, if you're concerned about your digital footprint on photographs that are emailed.

You should know, however, that when I upload photographs to Facebook, those photographs loose the digital information that was originally attached to the images, and that information is replaced by different digital information; namely a file number such as "41011_625658253525_672668527_5085837_5527822_n.jpg," which is Facebook's own file number for the image. Of course, that file number is linked to the Facebook account holder who uploaded the photo in the first place, allowing for the identification of the uploader by law enforcement agencies if the photograph involves a criminal act.

Readers should also be very concerned about "geotags," which are metadata embedded in photographs taken from GPS equipped smartphones and digital cameras. If activated on a phone or camera, it will identify the longitude and latitude of where the photograph was taken by the use of the device's GPS function. So if you take a picture of your house, your car, or your kids, the geotag metadata can and will reveal the latitude and longitude of where the photo was taken, potentially revealing your residence and other personal information about where you live and work. When latitude and longitude coordinates are inserted into search engines such as Google Street View, anyone (including thieves and stalkers) can identify your actual street address.

In addition to this information being embedded within metadata on photographs sent by email, geotagged images can be uploaded to sites such as Twitter, YouTube, Flickr, and Craigslist without the uploader having any idea that his or her location is contained (and traceable) in the image. This actually happened to Adam Savage, host of the popular *Mythbusters* television program, who posted a photograph of his car (a Toyota Land Cruiser) on Twitter, allowing two of his fans to find his residential address by the latitude and longitude unknowingly embedded in the image's metadata. They inserted that information into Google Street View, and found exactly where he lived. Savage's picture showed the car in front of his home, which is bad enough, but what if the geotagged image uploaded to Twitter, YouTube, Flickr, or Craigslist shows the location of a person's kids, their school, and places they regularly go for recreation? Doesn't this information make it all the easier for unscrupulous people to locate you and your family members? Or stalk you? Or know when you're not at home?

Allowing your camera or phone to reveal your location with geotags is not safe, but it's not easy to disable the geotag function in these devices. Disabling the geotag function often involves going through several layers of complicated menus on your device, until you find the location, GPS, or geotag setting, then hitting "off" or "don't allow." But doing this can sometimes deactivate the other reason you have GPS on your device; the GPS mapping function. If you want to disable this geotag function, *The New York Times* recommends ICanStalkU.com, which will give you instructions for disabling the geotag function for photographs on your iPhone, BlackBerry, Android, and Palm devices.

Metadata-scrubbing software is available online at Workshare.com, BatchPurifier by DigitalConfidence.com, and 3BClean at 3BView.com. There are more companies that offer this service and you can find them by simply putting "metadata removal software" in Google and investigating the numerous products available.

2. Word Documents

Just like there's metadata behind a digital image or photograph that remains with the image even though it's been dragged to another computer or emailed, documents contain metadata, particularly documents created in Microsoft Word and other word processing programs.

More than likely, you and your employees regularly send MS Word or other word-processed documents as email attachments. What you may or may not know is that the recipients of those emails (and subsequent recipients) can examine those email attachments to discover the author's name, tracked changes before the version has been sent, imbedded comments, and other information; some of it having the potential to be embarrassing, if not compromising.

You and your employees have undoubtedly sent correspondence, quotes, invoices, and deal sheets by email. If there are any negotiations between you and a client or supplier, you may have sent a letter of intent, a memorandum of understanding, or another document as an email attachment in Microsoft Word or other format, with the knowledge that the other person will be able to insert comments, or otherwise suggest changes to the document so the parties can get it to a point where the lawyers get involved (if the transaction is large enough to warrant it). Hopefully, both parties have used features such as Word's "track changes" function or DeltaView to allow you to see the other party's changes and to allow the other party to see yours.

If you're simply sending Word documents by email holus-bolus without thinking that the other party won't modify the document without telling you, guess again. Until I represented her, a client of mine used to send her franchise agreements out to franchisees in MS Word to print out, and return the executed hard copies to her. I got involved because one of her prospective franchisees had surreptitiously changed some of the essential terms of the agreement without her consent (i.e., the length of the term, the renewal right, and the royalty rate). The franchisee had made these changes in the same font and font size as the original document, and had signed and returned the hard copy of the contract without advising the franchisor of the modifications, or highlighting them in any way. He just hoped she wouldn't look. Needless to say, when she asked me what to do, I told her, "Sometimes bad faith just hits you in the face. Do you really want to be in business with someone who would pull that stunt on you?" Thankfully, the deal died.

However, the words within a document emailed around the planet are just part of the problem. You have to see a document as containing *more* than just words. You have to be very concerned about the metadata in the document.

The easiest way to explore the metadata behind a Word document is to see the document's "properties"; you can do this by going to the File toolbar and selecting "Properties" from the drop down menu.

In circumstances where a business is negotiating a contract with the supplier of certain components needed to build a product, or in any exchange of documents by email where one side wants to sell something and the other side wants to buy, letters of intent, memoranda of understanding, or proposals containing "deal points" will be transmitted back and forth. If your business just received a proposal from "Tony's Law Office" in Word, and you wanted to know more about the metadata behind the document, you'd go to File>Properties.

What would you do if you found this in the document's "properties"?

| General | Summary | Statistics | Contents | Custom |

Title: deal points - December 1, 2011

Subject: Cost Estimate for Sales - Preliminary Position

Author: D. Smith

Manager: Tony Wilson

Company: Tony's Law Office

Category:

Keywords:

Comments: opening position only - Rob says we can probably bend on items 2 and 3 if pressed. Confidential!

Hyperlink base:

Template: Normal.dotm

☑ Save preview picture with this document

Cancel   OK

This would tell you a lot, wouldn't it? Tony's Law Office is the company you're dealing with and probably all the software licenses in their office are identified in the same manner. D. Smith presumably typed the document, but conceivably it doesn't have to have been her, It could have been someone at her workstation.

It also appears she reports to Tony Wilson. However, note the subject of the document is revealed as "preliminary position," so if you receive this document, open it, and look at the metadata, you'll know that this isn't Tony's Law Office's final position. You can push them. Better yet, someone (perhaps the person who prepared the document), has repeated his or her instructions and has made a notation in the comments section:

"Opening position only — Tony says we can probably bend on items 2 and 3 if pressed. Confidential!"

Alternatively, you might find that the document wasn't authored by the person you're dealing with at Tony's Law Office, and the metadata might reveal the document originated from a company that isn't the company you're even dealing with. In other words, Tony's Law Office acquired the original electronic document from somewhere else (perhaps from another party on another deal), and modified it to suit their needs.

In some circumstances, you can see the changes made and accepted to an electronic document emailed to you going back all the way from the date the original document was created. This can be done by accessing the track changes function and going "back" as far as you can. If, after reviewing the tracked changes in a document, the author chose "final" in the reviewing toolbar instead of "accept all changes," the recipient of the document could click "original showing markup" and see the history of all the changes made. This might reveal different terms, different pricing, and other highlighted changes made to the document before it was emailed to you, and reveal the persons who reviewed the document. Or you might notice there are still comments embedded in the document when you hit the "comments" function.

Although not a part of "tracked changes," I've heard of some documents having comments made in white text in order to hide the words from everyone except the author. Of course, if the color of the font is changed, the white text is exposed. What can be worse is thinking you're hiding portions of text by highlighting words or sentences in black using the highlight function. Although this might look secure at first glance (and somewhat like bits of it have been crossed out with a thick black felt pen by a censor), all the reader has to do is re-highlight the words covered up, click yellow highlighting, or even better, no highlighting, and you'll see what the not-so-smart censor tried to cross out.

For the recipient of a document that hasn't had the metadata scrubbed, the ability to see previous tracked changes, deletions, imbedded comments, and white text might be a windfall in terms of positions to take in negotiations. If you are the sender, well, you might think your organization has a mole or a spy in it, and look to John le Carré novels for guidance.

Metadata isn't just a business risk. For teachers and university instructors, metadata in an essay or assignment can reveal that the purported author of the assignment wasn't the student enrolled in the class, but someone else, such as a commercial essay-preparation company or another student. Metadata can reveal plagiarism and other academic offenses.

Politicians have failed to appreciate the importance of metadata. The so-called "Downing Street memo" was downloaded in Microsoft Word from the British Prime Minister's website in 2002, revealing information for the justification of sending British troops to invade Iraq and depose Saddam Hussein. The memo had information "cut and pasted" from an American graduate student's work without referring to the student's work. The appearance was that justification for Britain's entry into the war was dictated by Washington, and that the highest office in the UK simply parroted whatever the White House told it to say.

In 2002, a lawyer I know was shocked to learn a securities filing he was involved in drafting revealed his "hidden" comments in the version of the prospectus filed with the TSX by another lawyer. The TSX was good enough to call the lead lawyer and alert her to the problem. A note to all the litigation lawyers out there, the metadata behind a document is discoverable in litigation proceedings.

Although sending documents as email attachments in portable document format (PDF) is far superior to sending documents in Word, some metadata can survive a conversion of a Word document to PDF, sometimes revealing tracked changes and other information. Scanning a document to PDF, however, will not transfer the metadata, and neither will faxes.

The answer to all this lies in using special software to scrub the metadata from the document before the document is emailed, prompting you to hit "scrub" or "don't scrub" each time you email a document.

If transmitting documents by email is a function of your business, unless you scrub your document clean of metadata, the recipients of your documents can learn a lot more about your document, your business, and you than you might want.

9
REPUTATION MANAGEMENT, SOCIAL MEDIA, AND YOUR BUSINESS

In 2008, a few of Virgin Atlantic Airlines' stewards posted very un-complimentary comments about Virgin's airplanes and its passengers on Facebook, including comments that the planes "were full of cock-roaches." To have posted these comments on Facebook was bad enough, but the comments became widely circulated in the media. Result? Thir-teen stewards were fired and Virgin's reputation was tarnished.

In 2007, John Mackey, who was at that time the President of Whole Foods, blogged under a pseudonym, and made some very un-complimentary comments about his competitor, Wild Oats Market, Inc., during merger negotiations between the companies. However, his posts were discovered, forcing him to resign as President.

There's the story from 2008 about a public relations executive who tweeted to his followers as soon as he got off a plane in Memphis, "I would die if I had to live here." Of course, the PR executive didn't realize that Memphis was the head office of FedEx, which was one of his company's largest clients, and FedEx found out about the tweet.

The Israeli army called off an incursion into a West Bank village because a soldier revealed on Facebook his combat unit, the location of the operation, and when the operation was to begin! He said, "On Wednesday we clean up Katana and on Thursday, God willing, we go home." His Facebook post was discovered by other members of his unit. The soldier was court-martialed and sentenced to ten days in jail.

Lastly, Lady Shelley Sawers, the wife of the Director of M16, Britain's Secret Intelligence Service, made postings to Facebook about her husband, their family, and their social and professional circle, which exposed potentially compromising details about where they lived and worked, who their "friends" were, and where they went on holiday. Lady Sawers put no privacy protection on the account, and any of Facebook's then 200 million users could see all her posts, no matter what terrorist organization the users belonged to.

So what do you do if statements are made by your employees on Facebook, Twitter, or on a blog that shouldn't be made? It may not be as serious as alerting terrorists on Facebook where you plan to take your holidays like Lady Sawers did, or reveal what town your army unit was about to secretly enter. However, in the world of business, there are many other mistakes that can seriously jeopardize your company, its reputation, and the relationships it has with its customers.

What if there's a blackout period where no public statements can be made about a company under securities laws? What if someone in your organization is using Facebook, Twitter, or other social media sites to promote a stock (and sell on the high) or trash a stock? What if technical resource people within a company are going back and forth on Facebook to a point where a potential patent application is jeopardized because the information is spotted by someone else and a patent application is made first? These transgressions might be innocent but have grave consequences.

What if an employee's posts to a social network site are disparaging and, perhaps, defamatory to your business or tarnish your company's reputation? What if disparaging comments made by employees on a blog or on Facebook complain about the company's hiring practices, human rights practices, workplace safety, sexual harassment on the job, hiring practices (e.g., only good looking girls need apply here), and other information which may open up a hornet's nest of legal consequences? Or the employees' comments may be vindictive about their place of employment and particularly toward those who hired them (and who, incidentally, pay their salaries)?

Like it or not, social media is here to stay. Registered users on Facebook number more than 500 million, making it the third largest country in the world, if it were a country. Banning social media use by a company's employees might well drive creative, expressive young people to companies that are more in tune with their thinking. In other words, you'll lose talent if you ban your employees from participating in social media. So you have to live with it and learn how to deal with it.

1. Why Social Media Is Important for Your Business

Social networking has extremely important business benefits. In many companies, social interaction between employees and persons outside of the company are essential, not only for happy employees you want to keep working for you, but for the strengthening of professional and business relationships between employees. Social networks such as LinkedIn and Facebook allow employees to expand their professional networks, get answers to specific questions quickly, and promote other aspects of the business such as products and services, competition, new technology, recruitment, and other information.

Arguably, social networks can help create what might be called a "back channel" for dialogue between colleagues. Indeed, you can indirectly "conference" on Facebook and other platforms between friends, so important information can be obtained from friends and colleagues almost instantaneously.

Company blogs and social networks are now regularly used to recruit new employees and contractors. For instance, recruiting information can be posted on Facebook, LinkedIn, or other similar sites. Applications for employment can be solicited on social networks and then this information can be obtained from potential candidates from around the world. In my limited experience on Facebook, I've seen at least three queries from "friends" who have said, "We have a job opening up in our company for a person with these sorts of skills. If you're interested, send a message to me immediately and I'll let you know where to apply."

One of these friends had upward of 400 friends in the media, public relations, and publishing industry. Any one of her circle who saw the post might have been interested and applied immediately. Or, if he or she wasn't interested in the job, he or she may have passed it on to someone who may have been interested.

From a recruiting perspective, blogs and participation by a company's employees in social networks may well help potential applicants get a real sense of "what the company is all about" and whether it's the right fit for them (and whether they are a right fit for the company). Arguably, blogs and social networks are excellent ways to either recruit new employees directly, or stimulate interest in your employee's circle of hopefully talented friends in your company. Of course, you don't have to necessarily do this on Facebook or LinkedIn; there could be specific blogs with respect to the company and employment opportunities, forms, lists, forums, and newsgroups.

2. The Importance of Setting Social Media Policies for Your Business

There are dangers involved in using social media. Posts, photographs, or other online commentary might be used to support litigation against your company by a competitor or an aggrieved consumer. As well, disclosure of certain issues on Facebook, blogs, Twitter, online forums, or elsewhere might accidentally disclose confidential information or trade secrets about the company or of others where the company and its employees must maintain confidentiality.

Disclosure on Facebook, LinkedIn, Twitter, or other social media sites might breach privacy laws by the disclosure of confidential personal information such as birthdays, religion, ethnicity, sexual orientation, medical conditions, and other information that businesses are required by law not to disclose and keep protected. Employees might get their employers into considerable difficulty if employees defame other employees of the company online during work hours, or they may defame customers or the employees of competitors. They may do it when not on company time as well.

If comments are made about another company on a social network site, and these are disparaging, or bring that company or its management or employees into disrepute, this may give rise to legal actions for defamation.

So no matter what type of business you have, you should formulate policies that your employees and contractors must adhere to as a condition of their employment regarding social media use.

A social media policy can't be limited to the general terms of "use of the Internet" or "use of Facebook." You have to be more specific in the terms of use of present and future technologies such as the following:

- Email communications and the use of the Internet generally on company-owned computers and devices such as cell phones. What shouldn't be said in an email or in a text

- Use of internal company Intranets

- Chat and Instant Messaging (IM) and what should and should not be said

- Blogs

- Social networking sites such as Facebook, MySpace, LinkedIn, etc.

- Communication by way of cell phones, iPhones, BlackBerries, and other wireless devices

- Use of cameras within cell phones

- Use of company laptops

- Use of software within cell phones or applications on Facebook or other social media sites that identify where you are through geo-tracking, geotags, or other systems

You may want to consider the following when drafting a social media policy:

- Notwithstanding the fact social media is here to stay, and notwithstanding my earlier comments that you have to live with it, you might very well want a policy that totally bans social media use (personally and in the office) if you're in the business of defense contracting, counter-terrorism, nuclear weapons development, espionage, biotechnology, the Mafia, or some other highly secretive business where information is very important to protect and dangerous if it gets out. By the way, the US Army allows its soldiers to post on Facebook; they just have policies regarding what can and can't be said, and all the soldiers know what they post is monitored. So, monitoring may be the thing that keeps employees on the right track.

- Company servers can block Facebook, LinkedIn, and other sites to prohibit access from employees from company computers. However, laptops, notebook computers, and especially iPhones, BlackBerrys, Androids, and other smartphones that can link to the Internet through 3G or Wi-Fi networks in coffee shops, from home, at airports, or virtually anywhere, can effectively go around company servers. An employee can easily post a status update through his or her iPhone or iPod Touch. If you're going to outright prohibit social networking in the office, you really have to consider how you will monitor it and enforce it given how prevalent and easy it has become.

- You may want to have rules about postings that emanate from computers or smartphones owned by your company and used by employees. That is to say, your policy may be "If you're going to do it, do it at home on your own time, and on your own computer, but not on office time on office devices." As long as employees know that this is the policy and that serious consequences will flow from noncompliance, they've been warned.

If you do permit employees to engage in social networking from work (or on company-owned handheld devices), you may want to limit the employees' comments and conduct to something that is related to work. Or you may want to permit some limited personal use; the way you might with personal telephone calls (e.g., the occasional one is fine).

Whether employees are at work or at home, do you want to have a policy that prohibits identifying the employees' employment with that employer? That is to say, he or she can't say that they work for BP, Boeing, the FBI, or any other company or organization that might not want their brand mentioned on social media sites. You might say, "Post what you want, but be professional. No one can know who your employer is online, and if you do disclose it, you will be fired."

You might allow social media use by employees for "appropriate business purposes." How do you define those purposes? It might be appropriate for people in the restaurant business to go back and forth on Facebook. I'm not comfortable with doctors, lawyers, or accountants having professional business exchanges on social media, other than, "Have you read that new Supreme Court case that came out today?" It comes down to the appropriateness of the communication in the context of the job.

Consider how to manage what is said about your company online and whether you have the resources to manage what your employees and customers say about your company. If you're going to outright prohibit social networking in the office, how will you monitor it? Should you have a person in your organization who is designated as the "social media tsar," who is responsible for managing business content on social media sites, and managing what employees say about the company, what the public says about the company, and the ongoing reputation of the company online?

I'd say it would be difficult if not impossible to monitor social network use by employees without someone in the organization whose job it is to do this. Frankly, there is no point in having a policy with respect to email, Internet use, and social media use if you're not going to monitor your employees. Your policy should indicate that emails going through company servers will be randomly checked. Hard drives may be checked on a random basis for appropriate content, and blogs and other social media posts may be monitored by the company.

• Consider how you will enforce the social media use policy in the workplace. You may need to train your managers to implement the policy.

Perhaps employees recognize that all hardware and software owned by the company is the property of the company and all data may be inspected at any time by representatives of the company. If it's your computer, you have the right to see what's on it and what's on it should be for business purposes only. Same thing for your server. You may also want to monitor what goes through your broadband.

Certain information that employees are exposed to may be confidential trade secrets. It's a good idea to have written employment contracts or contractor agreements that contain covenants of confidentiality and nondisclosure. By ensuring that your employees and contractors are contractually bound to covenants of confidentiality, you will have some legal recourse against the employee or contractor in the event that confidential information belonging to your business is distributed to others or otherwise disclosed.

Use of material downloaded from the Internet onto computers and other devices within the office, and distributing this information might also be a violation of another person's copyright to that material. An example might be finding a contract on the Web between two high-tech companies, and downloading that contract for use in another deal. Or by using a company's operations manual found on the Web, by downloading it and changing names so that it can be used for your company. Sometimes I'll get a new client with a problem with his or her contract, and part of the problem is that it's copied from another contract from the Internet (a breach of copyright, at the very least) without changing some of the names and deal terms.

You should seek to identify inappropriate sites and block those sites from company servers (e.g., pornographic sites, eBay, Craigslist, gaming sites, or other personal sites).

3. Social Media and Internet Policies for Employees at Home

The guidelines for social media and Internet policies noted above relate to the use of social media and other forms of communication either at the office, on office devices, or at the office on company time. What about after-hours use of social media? Consider the following questions:

- Should your employees be posting about "drinking binges" on Facebook or tweeting about the bender they're on via Twitter for all their friends (and your customers) to see?

- Should the employees be joining inappropriate groups that are publicly viewable to others on a social network?

- What about blogging or making other commentary that has nothing to do with their work at the office but may nonetheless affect your reputation as their employer?

- What about photographs tagged by others?

The difficulty here is the balance that must be done between the employer's right to expect certain standards of behavior from employees, and the employees' right to live their lives the way they see fit.

Following are two sample policies you might want to consider using in your organization. Sample 1 is a "technology use policy" I'm preparing for my 120-person law office. Sample 2 is a basic social media policy that includes guidelines for participation in social networks.

Sample 2 may not be applicable to your business or even your industry. A law firm has to consider client confidentiality and the requirements of its law society or other governing body; so arguably, these guidelines might be on the tougher end of the spectrum. However, this is a good place to start.

ABC LAW CORPORATION TECHNOLOGY USE POLICY

This policy applies to everyone who works at or for ABC Law Corporation ("ABC").

Application

This policy covers the use of any technology owned, leased, or licensed by ABC, including computers, printers, photocopiers, fax machines, scanners, telephones, cellular phones, smartphones, personal digital assistants, and any other electronic devices that can create, copy, store, record, send, or receive information to or from another electronic device (all of which is referred to below as "ABC Technology").

Personal Use

Unless otherwise agreed upon, ABC Technology is intended for company business use only and not for your personal use. You may make reasonable personal use of the office telephones, email, and computer access to the Internet if you do so with discretion, i.e., avoid personal use during normal working hours (except for emergencies), keep it short, ensure that it does not interfere with the performance of your work or the work of others, do not make personal long-distance calls, stay away from any controversial, disparaging, or offensive content that might reflect badly on you or on the company, do not use it for your own business purposes, etc.

Personal use is a privilege, not a right. Be careful not to abuse it. We reserve the right, at our sole discretion, to restrict, suspend, or terminate that privilege.

Email Communications

To avoid the risk of having an email communication or attached document modified without your consent, these types of communications should be sent in a PDF format and a hard copy version retained in the file.

Email can be a very informal medium for "chatting." Caution should be exercised on how it is to be used in reference to any client matters. Any email you send is a written communication that may later be retrieved and be used as evidence in a legal proceeding.

Notification of Monitoring

ABC Technology, including the computer storage, email, voicemail, and Internet access systems, is not private. We reserve the right to monitor and review, at our sole discretion, any ABC Technology, including the email and voicemail systems or the addresses of any websites you have visited, at any time and to review, copy, or delete any material that does not comply with this policy. Monitoring may include content, volume, or other matters by manual or electronic means related to use of ABC Technology. This monitoring is to ensure compliance with this policy and to assist ABC in fulfilling its legal obligations regarding any inappropriate use of its technology.

Prohibitions

Do not use any ABC Technology for your own business purposes, gambling or betting, or accessing, displaying, viewing, recording, scanning, photocopying, sending, or receiving any content that is X-rated, pornographic, hateful, discriminatory, or demeaning.

Do not access other people's email, voicemail, or private directories without their prior knowledge and consent unless it is required to obtain client information or carry out client instructions or is authorized by the Board of Directors.

Do not allow anyone who is not authorized to have access to or use any ABC Technology (except the telephone for local calls) without the prior approval of the Board of Directors and the appropriate supervision.

Avoid copyright infringement. If you are in doubt as to whether you have the right to copy or use certain material, confer with the Board of Directors before proceeding.

Restricted Uses

You should not, without prior approval from the Board of Directors —

- use the Internet to play; download; or record music, radio, or video services. This "streaming" use results in higher usage costs;

- store any personal data files on the network hard drives;

- download any software or executable files from the Internet that are not business-related — it may contain a virus and may not be compatible with other programs on your workstation;

- open any attachment to an email message that is from an unknown or uncertain source or access any external email account (e.g., Hotmail, Yahoo!). This is to avoid the risk of a virus getting into our system;

- install any software that is not licensed to ABC due to the risk of copyright infringement; or

- give any password or log-on information or access code to any unauthorized person.

Effect of Noncompliance

Failure to comply with the provisions of this technology use policy may result in disciplinary action, suspension, or termination.

ABC LAW CORPORATION SOCIAL NETWORKING POLICY

First of all, we have no objection to you creating or participating on blogs or other social networks. We appreciate how valuable social networking can be among our employees, and we also appreciate that this is the way many people communicate now. Online social networking and use of social media is changing the way people work, and we realize that it allows for new ways to engage with friends and colleagues. However, if you create your own blog or make a comment on someone else's blog, post a LinkedIn profile, use Facebook to post status updates or communicate with friends, or you participate in any other online social media (i.e., Twitter, wikis, blogs, chat rooms, Internet forums, electronic mailing lists, or ones that we haven't named but which will no doubt arise in the future) and your profile identifies you as working for ABC Law Corporation, you have to be aware that your activities online may be associated with our law firm. If your online comments or conduct (including the posting of videos or photographs) are inappropriate or offensive in any way, this may affect the reputation of our law firm, our lawyers, and our clients. Because you work at a law firm, we believe you have to be very aware of the nature of what you post, and the consequences of posting the wrong thing.

Whether you're a lawyer or a valuable staff member, your use of social media should adhere to the following guidelines:

1. First and foremost, you always have to maintain client confidentiality in compliance with our confidentiality policies. Do not identify clients or matters that you are working on that might, directly or indirectly, reveal the identity of a client.

2. If you're going to write something in your blog, or make a comment on Facebook, or Tweet, or communicate publically in any other manner, don't give "advice" that might be construed as legal advice on any particular set of facts or ask specific questions that might inadvertently establish a solicitor-client relationship with that person.

3. Don't post or publish anything that you would not want to be viewed by anyone who has access to the Internet. Remember, clients, potential clients, potential employees, new lawyers and opposing counsel may look for our firm and our lawyers online. They may make judgments about our firm and about you based on what they see online. So remember, don't be rude or offensive, and don't post anything that you wouldn't want your supervisor, or your most important client to see. This includes photographs.

4. Many people don't understand the privacy settings in Facebook and other social networking sites. Understand these policies so that you know what is private between your friends, and what might be viewable by "friends of friends" you don't know. Be cognizant of protecting your own privacy, and always have an interest in protecting your own reputation from harm.

5. Although freedom of speech is a right we all cherish, be aware that some comments can be harmful, offensive, inappropriate, or embarrassing to you, to the people you may be commenting about, and the firm. Know that some comments (or conduct) on Facebook and other social media sites may be defamatory.

6. [Optional] If you are commenting on a topic related exclusively to your work, identify yourself as a lawyer or an employee, as the case may be. Be transparent and don't hide what you are. If you are a lawyer, you may link to your profile on the firm's website. However, make it clear that you are expressing views that are your own and not necessarily those of the firm and that you are not giving legal advice.

7. Perception is often reality. Recognize that the lines between your public and private life, and between your personal and professional life can overlap and be fuzzy. By participating in social networking, you may be creating perceptions about your professional life by revealing aspects of your personal life.

8. Again, be sensitive to how your comments may be viewed by clients of the firm. Be respectful of your colleagues, the firm, our competitors, and the legal profession.

9. Do not use any firm logos or trademarks. This is the firm's intellectual property and is not to be used without the firm's consent.

10. Don't infringe on anyone else's copyright. This includes copyright in photographs. Don't post photographs without the consent of the person in the photograph.

11. Do not expect anonymous postings to stay anonymous. The law in this area has changed and your anonymity is not protectable.

12. Get approval from the Executive before you launch any blog that is related to your work and which uses our name, logo, or trademarks.

13. From time to time, we may access and read what you post online to ensure that it complies with these guidelines.

Act reasonably and responsibly online! And think before you post!

4. Monitor What Is Said about Your Business

Your company, your brand, and your products or services are being talked about every day by someone; if you're lucky, by a lot of people and it will all be favorable.

Tweets can just as easily damage your reputation as something said in a newspaper, a magazine, or on a blog. Shaw Communications recently launched a lawsuit in British Columbia Supreme Court against Novus Entertainment and 6S Marketing Inc. for what was described by Shaw Communications as "a campaign of disseminating and publishing defamatory and false statements" about Shaw and the products that it offers. Novus engaged in an advertising campaign to use social marketing and tweets on Twitter to divert business to Novus, based on Shaw's pricing policies, which Novus described as "predatory."

There are numerous cases in the United States that have involved allegedly defamatory tweets posted on Twitter. The entertainment blogger Perez Hilton was threatened with legal action by actor Demi Moore with respect to tweets made by Hilton. Courtney Love, the widow of Nirvana rock star Kurt Cobain, made allegations on Twitter that a particular fashion designer was a liar and a thief. A US chain of pizza restaurants whose marketing company made posts on Facebook and Twitter was hit with a $2 million lawsuit for the comments it made.

How do you *monitor* what is being said by others in the blogosphere or otherwise on the Internet about you, your company, your brand, or your product?

One way to monitor what people might be saying about you or your business is to simply use the advanced search section of Google. For example, if you want to see what people are saying about you or your business online, simply put your business name, product name, or brand name in the space for "this exact wording or phrase."

If you're an established company, there may be dozens if not hundreds of "hits" that cause you to dig deeper and determine whether the comments are made about your company or about someone else's. Some of the results may be generated by your company itself, if your business has an online presence (e.g., your business's website, advertisements).

You might be able to weed through some of your own content and discover what people are saying about your company and brand.

There may even be situations where a customer tweets something about your company and you might want to respond to it directly.

Frankly, I don't find this to be wholly effective. A better solution to monitor your company name, brand, products, or for that matter your own name, is to use Google Alerts to do it for you automatically, and to send you daily, weekly, or "as it happens" alerts to your inbox every time Google runs across your name, brand, or product on the Web. As I write for a number of print and online newspapers and magazines, some of these articles find their way all over the world onto websites in Australia, India, and elsewhere in Asia I didn't know existed, so I'm interested in where my articles go, and what the articles now say (i.e., have they been edited without me knowing?), and if there is online commentary about one of my pieces that I should know about. I know (because a web analytics expert ran the numbers and told me so) that a piece I wrote for *The Globe and Mail* in July 2009 went viral, appearing on websites all over the world. Think of what people could be saying about your brand and products all over the world.

In Google Alerts put the words you want alerts on (e.g., your name, your company's name, your product's name) in quotes so Google picks up the exact word combination, but refine it further by adding a modifier word to the search criteria that relates to your business sector, and Google will email you an alert when those words show up on the Web. If I want to get a Google alert regarding a use of my name in conjunction with law, I'll put my name in quotes, followed by the word *law*. If I want to see my name in association with things I've written for *The Globe and Mail*, I'll put the "Globe and Mail" in the search parameters in quotes, but separate from my name in quotes. It's easy to do for your business as well. It's also easy to see what people are saying about your competitors in the same way. Just use their names in Google Alerts in the same manner.

You might also find comments made by your employees on blogs, forums, and Twitter about you and your company. Or if you're a teacher or college or university professor, from your students who may have made unflattering comments about you and your teaching.

You might find favorable (or unfavorable) comments posted on sites such as TripAdvisor, restaurant or product review forums, and other sites where customers are asked to rate and give comments on a product or service. Note that consumers will make comments, and often; especially upset consumers.

The point is this: How do you know your business is being reviewed or otherwise commented on negatively unless you are monitoring your brand name or product name on the Web?

As stated above, you can use something as simple as Google Alerts, but you can also subscribe to Google Reader and Google Blog Search in your monitoring. Yahoo! Alerts is another automatic monitoring service similar to Google Alerts, in which words or phrases (including company names, brands, products etc.) can be entered into the Yahoo! search engine, and the service will notify you when the word or phrase combination is found. Omgili (an acronym for "Oh my God I love it") is another search engine for finding communities, message boards, and discussion threads about any topic, which might be about your business, your products, or your competition. These aren't the only services you can use to monitor your reputation or the reputation of your company, but they are a good start.

Using these types of sites to search the Web for your company or product name might also reveal trademark use by infringers who are using your brand without your knowledge or consent, negative feedback and commentary, positive feedback and commentary, as well as websites that are created specifically to besmirch and degrade your company or brand (e.g., NikeSucks).

Now that I've given you reasons why you should monitor your reputation and some tools to help you monitor it, what can (and should) you do about negative publicity online? Well, as a lawyer I can tell you you shouldn't launch a defamation or other legal action except as a last resort. It can seriously backfire. By way of example, Horizon Realty Group of Chicago sued its former tenant, Amanda Bonnen, for $50,000 over a single tweet. Bonnen's tweet read: "Who said sleeping in a moldy apartment was bad for you? Horizon realty thinks it's okay." The tweet was found, because Horizon was monitoring all uses of the word Horizon on the Web (which included Bonnen's Twitter account as she mentioned the brand Horizon). She wasn't a heavy Twitter user, posting between one and five tweets per day to her 20 followers.

But here's the thing to know about starting lawsuits against people who say things about you online. They can backfire, very badly.

Horizon's lawsuit against its former tenant had a negative backlash. Although a representative of Horizon, Jeffrey Michael, stated, "We're a sue first, ask questions later kind of organization," suing a tenant over a tweet as opposed to dealing with a customer complaint arising from a tweet can (and did) backfire badly. Horizon's lawsuit received considerable negative publicity in the Chicago area, causing Michael to apologize on the Web about his approach to suing a former tenant.

So, if you want to attract bad publicity or otherwise get reported in the mainstream press as a big company throwing its weight (and legal resources) around, consider a legal action. However, if you want to win over a disgruntled customer, and perhaps attract new ones, you have to think smarter, and not always go running to your lawyer.

By way of example, the Insurance Corporation of British Columbia (ICBC), which runs most of the automobile insurance in the province, uses services such as Google Alerts to monitor the acronym ICBC. Said one person on Twitter who made a claim with ICBC:

"Picking up my car later today from Kirmac ... finally! Oh and, screw you ICBC!"

Shortly after this tweet was posted, an employee of ICBC tweeted back to him, and said, "Hi [name withheld] it seems you're unhappy with us. Anything I can do to help?"

A bit shocked that ICBC saw his tweet, he replied, "ICBC for real? On Twitter ... LOL, it's all good nothing can really be done now."

There's a couple of lessons to be learned in this excerpt. First, your tweets can be discovered by anyone looking for certain phrases or buzz words including brands and trademarks. In this example, ICBC wanted to see what people were saying about its brand. It monitored all online use of the term ICBC and discovered this individual's tweet. Note that ICBC wasn't a follower of this individual, but the ICBC employee simply found the tweet online, probably by use of Google Alerts or a similar service.

The second point to learn from this exchange is that this was a marvelous example of good customer service. ICBC saw a claimant that was unhappy and wanted to know if it could help. The claimant, dumbfounded that his tweet was discovered, seemed to backpedal and say everything was okay. It's a good reason to use services such as Google Alerts to monitor what people are saying about your brand, if not for any other reason, to see if you can help an aggrieved customer. ICBC had the opportunity to make it right with the customer.

Online commentary might not be defamatory at all. The negative comments may have been made out of frustration, and the criticism may be well deserved. But finding the comment and addressing it from a customer service perspective might be an opportunity to make an unhappy customer a happy one. Maybe the product is defective. Or maybe the customer hasn't read the manual thoroughly and you have a chance to assist him or her online.

You can't always deal one-on-one with a disgruntled customer when you have thousands (or millions) of them. Perhaps the most obvious solution is to direct negative commentary directly to a page that you yourself control as part of your company's website. A discussion group page will allow consumers to ask questions (which you might be able to answer just by referring them to an FAQ page). Or technical people within the organization could answer the questions within the discussion group format. This gives representatives of your company feedback on whether a product is doing what it's supposed to be doing so that bugs can be detected and fixes undertaken to the product. If it's software, this may be solved by a downloadable patch. If it's something else, such as computer hardware, a vacuum cleaner, or a coffee maker that isn't working properly, consumer complaints via discussion groups may be the first point where the company gets wind of a defect, hopefully dealing with that defect by repair or replacement and improving the product for the next manufacturing cycle. In other words, use consumer information to make a better product for next time, while at the same time, ensuring the consumer is looked after in the here and now. Use commentary and criticism to be better at what you do.

Most manufacturers and distributors (certainly in the software business) will have internal discussion group pages. There may also be non-company sponsored forums in your industry where consumers comment, criticize, or complain about your product or service, or the products of others. If you are going to post responses, I think transparency is extremely important and if you're responding on an independent forum, you aren't pretending to be someone else. Say at the outset who you represent, treat the "poster" (no matter how irate he or she is) with respect and courtesy, and genuinely try to help. Otherwise don't do it at all.

Getting all your employees, friends, and relatives to surreptitiously say good things about you, your company, and your products on a forum or in a discussion group may well backfire if the context of the comments makes it apparent that the comments aren't from other users or consumers. If they are self-serving, likely identical in information, and not helpful, it makes it obvious the comments were posted by friends and family of the business owner.

The same is true for fake product reviews; that is, reviews that put a positive spin on a product or service where the reader believes the comment is coming from another consumer or expert. It's similar to astroturfing in the public relations business; that is, a PR company setting up what appears to be a grass-roots or ground-level organization that's really an apologist, promoter, and spinner for the industry that's funding it. Astroturfing organizations are often exposed, with embarrassing consequences. Fake reviews can be found and exposed as well. Don't do it. It's too easy to expose.

Negative comments on forums, websites, and blogs might be found faster on Google and other search engines than the responses you are providing to disgruntled consumers (if your comments are being found at all). Getting to the top of a Google search or on the first page of other search engines is indispensable in attracting new business, but it's just as indispensable in ensuring that your business's web page pops up in a search before the comments of the critics — in essence, burying the bad press. Hiring technical consultants experienced with Search Engine Optimization (SEO) may also be a solution to dealing with negative online commentary. There are ways of making sure that some pages rank in Google ahead of others, particularly by use of content and keywords.

You can hire a company to help you monitor and protect your company's name and reputation. For example, ReputationDefender will search for information about your business, and help you remove inappropriate, inaccurate, or otherwise slanderous information about you and your company. There are other commercial services that will assist.

4.1 Be aware of your identity, and who may be using it

It's one thing for a person to post sensitive, derogatory, or other information about his or her company or employer that may have legal repercussions. But what if someone is posting or otherwise going on social media pretending to be you? Michael Smith, the star of the

TV show *Chef at Home* discovered the hard way that tweets being sent out on Twitter under the name Chef_@_home were not from him even though they contained his picture. Tweets sent out under Chef_@_home attacked the food-service industry in Montreal. In a press release, Smith said the tweets were not from him and that he was very concerned about protecting his reputation. All this was discovered when a reporter from *The Gazette* interviewed Smith about tweets that attacked restaurants in Montreal where serving staff were called "sullen and bitter" and the food "grotesque and tragic."

Smith indicated that he is not on Twitter and that he is attempting to get his identity removed from the Twitter feed. He's also hired a company that will monitor his name and reputation in case it happens again.

10
SOCIAL MEDIA
CAMPAIGNS

If you're going to use social media to build a brand online, or to repair a reputation online during (or in anticipation of) a public relations crisis, there are a few things you might put want to think about doing in your venture into social media.

1. Try to Be Your Customers' Friend

You're not trying to sell your customers something, at least not directly. Although some people may care if chicken wings are 12 for $1.99 today, most people who follow you and your brand want to be engaged by you. They want to be interested in you and what you're doing. They want to know how you feel about things. So instead of trying to sell chicken wings for $1.99, maybe you want to have the customers decide whether your restaurant should serve Bellinis or Guinness on special.

Is there a hockey game on tonight? Have your Facebook fans bet on the score.

Is Arnold Schwarzenegger, Lady Gaga, or Harrison Ford in one of your restaurants for lunch? Well, when the celebrity leaves (and *only* when he or she leaves), post something about it on your Facebook Fan or Group page and send out a tweet to your followers. Nothing works like a celebrity in your establishment.

You want your fans to want to be attracted to your business. It's a romance, of sorts. Be their friend and, at times, be more than a friend. Don't be their pizza delivery person. Don't try to be a telemarketer. Don't be a car salesperson. Be their friend.

2. Find True Believers

Locate the people "in your corner" who believe in you, your company, your products, and what you're all about, especially in a crisis. Maybe they're customers with great things to say. Maybe they're suppliers. But they're out there, so find current or future "evangelists" who can validate and support you. Engage them and keep engaging them to build (or if necessary, defend) your reputation and your brand. Count on them when things go sour. Apple is a great example of a company with true believers.

3. Dedication and Commitment

We all know times are tough and money is tight, but if you're going to use social media to build or defend your reputation, you have to do it well, and often. If you're trying to build a brand online, or repair a reputation that's been damaged (either online or otherwise), and you want to use social media to get the message out, as Nike would say, "Just Do It."

If you're building a reputation and a brand, you should be engaging your followers regularly. You have to supply content regularly, especially if you're having a public relations challenge. A tweet a day won't cut it for Twitter followers and forgetting to update your Facebook page will serve to lose followers' interest.

For a real world example, Chronoswiss makes some of the most wonderful, desirable luxury watches in the world. I saw a Chronoswiss Opus in a watch store in Lugano, Switzerland, in 2006, and fell in love with it. My wife bought it for me in 2009 for Christmas, and I get nothing but compliments on it. That watch projects an image of me with which I identify. I am an evangelist for the brand. A true believer. But at the time of writing, Chronoswiss' Facebook page hadn't been updated with new information about the products or the brand for two years.

Now go to a restaurant chain in Vancouver called Cactus Club Cafe at its Facebook page.

It says in one post, "How would you describe Road 13's Rock-pile?" The Cactus club is asking its fans about a new Okanagan wine it's selling. Or it has "The stories behind the art in our restaurants."

Regular updates about drinks, wine, art, menu items, sports, what restaurant has the best bathrooms in town, and other engaging content keeps fans engaged, creates true believers, often amuses, and never blatantly tries to sell something.

4. Consider Using Different Types of Social Media

If Facebook were a country, it would be the third largest country in the world, but it's not the only place online that can fill a country. Some people refuse to go on it, and some people refuse to be followers of anyone on Twitter.

Although not strictly speaking social media, your business website can be made more engaging by adding blogs and other interesting content.

Consider email blasts through companies like Constant Contact to people who have voluntarily left their business cards at your office or at a trade show (say for a contest).

Consider updates on LinkedIn, which is where many professionals network (rather than on Facebook).

5. Don't Ignore What Your Customers Are Saying

Deal with customers when they say good things and when they say bad things — don't ignore them. Web 2.0 in general and social media in particular involves interaction. Unlike a web page, it's not one way. It's not static. You need to deal with people, and interact with them, particularly the ones who might contact you first online — either with a compliment or a criticism.

Don't ignore negative criticism. Always respond to every person who comments online. Your online reputation will benefit.

6. Monitor Your Influence on Twitter

If you're on Twitter, and you think tweets have a value, how do you gauge if you're influential, and that your tweets are being followed not just by followers, but by others? There are third-party applications such as Klout, TwitterGrader.com, and TwInfluence that will actually measure your influence by their own standard of influence, which is more than simply the number of people who follow you.

7. Monitor Conversations

Just like the example mentioned in Chapter 9 about ICBC following and reacting to a tweet from a dissatisfied customer, tweets that use a company's trademark or brand can be followed, through Google Alerts or other services. Monitor conversations using these applications and respond when you think it's appropriate. Again, try to help the customer and don't be critical. However, don't be surprised if someone is shocked that his or her tweets were being monitored.

8. Things Change So Be There When They Do

Look for more information about social media as much as you can, because things change, and you have to stay on top of it in order to benefit your business.

11
UNDERSTANDING PRIVACY POLICIES ON SOCIAL MEDIA SITES

This book has been written to give readers a general sense of the digital footprint they leave in the sand by their activities online, whether those activities are as innocent as sending an email with a photograph in it; posting photographs or videos to a social networking site; commenting about a person or a company in a blog, a forum, on Twitter, or on other digital media; posting status updates; or having online conversations with friends or colleagues. Virtually anything that is sent from a computer or smartphone to another computer or phone that is in text or which is in the form of a digital image can be retained within the receiver's computer or phone and recirculated to others, either one person at a time, or via social networks where the text or image can become distributed virally and be seen by millions. I have tried to instill in readers my view that online conduct is like a digital tattoo, traces of which may still remain with you even though you've tried to have that tattoo removed.

The online network that seems to get the most scrutiny respecting the conduct (or misconduct) of its users is Facebook. As I've said previously, as of September 2010, it had more than 500,000,000 registered users, making it the third largest country in the world, if it were a country; and 70 percent of its registered users were outside of the United States.

At one time, Facebook's largest competitor was MySpace, but at the time of writing this book, MySpace only had 66 million users. Former MySpace CEO, Owen Van Natta, admitted that MySpace's energies weren't served by going head-to-head with Facebook and that it had to find its own market niche in the social media milieu; that niche appeared to be geared to music and entertainment.

As for LinkedIn, those who use it know it's for business. It's an online résumé, a networking forum for people in business to connect with others in business, and in part, for people to post their credentials for customers, clients, competitors, and future employers to see. Reputation management issues aren't as prevalent on LinkedIn, because most people who are on it know that their customers, clients, competitors, and future employers are all on it as well. The demographics of the user base are quite different than Facebook's so as a social network, there are less "slip ups." Besides, when there's a news story about a policeman who has been suspended for sneaking an underage girl into a beer garden (representing that the girl was "of age" to the other authorities), that officer was exposed because pictures were posted on Facebook, not LinkedIn. It's Facebook that movies are made about.

So it's Facebook that's the phenomenon with half a billion users. It's Facebook where people and companies are making — and ruining — their online reputations. And it's Facebook which is pushing the law as far as it can go in terms of what information is private and what information isn't, testing the willpower of the Privacy Commissioner of Canada and those responsible for Privacy laws in Europe and elsewhere in the world, which have "pushed back" Facebook. Therefore, it's Facebook's privacy policy I want to look at; at least the policy that existed in September 2010.

Like the VCR in the '80s and '90s always blinking "12:00" because owners found setting the time on the device too complicated, many of the problems associated with reputation management since 2008 come from users either not caring about their online privacy on Facebook, or not knowing how to adjust their privacy settings on Facebook.

A few points about Facebook founder Mark Zuckerberg. First, in 2010, he was only 26 years old. It's an important fact to know. He may well be part of a generation that is less concerned about their digital footprint than those who are older. Second, he does not believe in privacy; at least to the extent others do. In an interview he gave in January 2010,

Zuckerberg declared that "the age of privacy was over" and that if he was creating Facebook again today, everything would be public. He said in a recent interview in *The New Yorker*, "A lot of people who are worried about privacy and those kinds of issues will take any minor misstep that we make and turn it into as big a deal as possible." Third, *The Social Network* may be a Hollywood film that didn't totally accurately portray Mr. Zuckerberg, but it wasn't totally inaccurate, either.

Now that you are armed with the knowledge that Facebook is only concerned about privacy when it's pushed, let's look at its policy.

1. Facebook's Privacy Policy

Facebook's privacy policy is easy to access, but it could change again by the time you read this. Simply log on to Facebook, scroll to the bottom of the page and click on the "Privacy" link and it will direct you to a page from which you can access not only the policy, but also privacy and safety information and resources. The following discussion is a brief overview of Facebook's privacy policy and how Facebook interacts with a user's information. Note that it changes from time to time.

In order to sign up for a Facebook account, users must provide four pieces of information about themselves: name, email, gender, and birth date. It is completely up to the user whether he or she wants to share any more information. Facebook justifies its need to collect the user's name, so others can find them, the user's email, so Facebook can contact them, and the user's age, because Facebook prohibits anyone younger than 13 from having a Facebook account. However, this doesn't stop people younger than 13 lying about their birth years. Also, Facebook doesn't indicate why gender is necessary.

The only portions of a Facebook profile that a person cannot hide are his or her name and profile picture. But if he or she doesn't post a profile picture, then this is effectively the same as hiding a picture. Facebook justifies this openness by referencing its commitment to the free flow of information.

When a user interacts with Facebook, Facebook collects certain information about that user. Facebook collects the user's site activity information, such as when a person adds a friend, joins a group, or connects to an application; as well as when a person accesses device and browser information, such as the browser type and location, IP address, and pages visited. Facebook will also place cookies on your computer that provide Facebook with information about you when you return in the future. This information helps Facebook target advertising based on your personal and geographical characteristics, so that advertisers can target you better so you might buy their stuff.

What you probably didn't realize is that Facebook also collects information about users from other users. Whenever another person tags a user in a photo or video or updates friend or relationship details involving that user, Facebook collects that information to understand both users and to reflect it in their profiles.

This leads to the next question: What does Facebook do with a user's information? Facebook uses this information to manage the services it provides to users. Facebook does this by contacting the user when appropriate, making suggestions such as friend suggestions, helping friends of a user find that person, and memorializing accounts when a user dies so that confirmed friends and family can post to the deceased user's wall.

Facebook also uses this information to provide value to its paying customers — advertisers. Advertisers provide Facebook with their target market, and Facebook utilizes the user's information to target applicable advertising toward that user. The more information a user provides on his or her profile, the more targeted and personalized the advertising. Facebook may also utilize a user's information to understand the effectiveness of advertising and improve the quality and targeting of ads. For example, if I say I like scuba diving, I'll see ads on the right-hand margin for "Dive Tours to the Red Sea." I've listed "shark diving" as one of my interests, and wouldn't you know it? Dive tours to see sharks are advertised. Likewise, if I like skiing, I'll see ski holidays advertised. If I indicate I am single, then I may see ads for singles' bars or singles' holidays. It's important to remember what you list as an "interest" or that what you "like" will trigger advertisements on the Facebook page you're looking at to target you with those kinds of ads. It's genius.

Furthermore, Facebook may keep information about the user. If a user deactivates his or her account or deletes the account or content, backup versions of the information may remain for a period of time. However, even if a user does delete or deactivate an account or deletes content, this account or content may still be available to others if another user has copied or stored it or if the user distributed the information to others (such as photographs).

Interestingly, if a user conducts a transaction or makes a payment on Facebook, it is Facebook's default setting to store that payment source account number. The user must actively set his or her payment's page to tell Facebook to delete this information.

There is even information that a user can never delete such as messages. If user A sends a message to user B, user A can delete it from his or her message outbox, but as long as user B keeps the message, the message continues to exist.

1.1 Facebook's statement of rights and responsibilities

Facebook's statement of rights and responsibilities governs Facebook's relationship with its users and others who interact with Facebook. Essentially, the statement is Facebook's terms of use and, if a person uses Facebook, he or she agrees to these terms.

The statement is important because it sets out the rights to a user's information including Facebook's use of that information. You can find the most important part of the statement under the heading "Sharing Your Content and Information." Facebook says the following:

"You own all of the content and information you post on Facebook, and you can control how it is shared through privacy and application settings." In addition:

"For content that is covered by intellectual property rights, like photos and videos ('IP Content'), you specifically give us the following permission, subject to your privacy and application settings: you grant us a non-exclusive, transferable, sub-licensable, royalty-free, worldwide license to use any IP content that you post on or in connection with Facebook ('IP License'). This IP License ends when you delete your IP content or your account unless your content has been shared with others, and they have not deleted it [emphasis added]." This is important because, while a user maintains actual ownership of all IP Content, Facebook has essentially used this clause to grant to itself the majority of rights associated with ownership of your intellectual property.

Another interesting point is that it is against Facebook's terms of use for a user to provide any false personal information, such as a false name, and a user must keep his or her contact information current and accurate.

The statement governs other areas, one of which is safety. This section requires users to agree not to bully, not to post offensive content, and not to use Facebook to do anything unlawful, misleading, malicious, or discriminatory. Another area is not infringing another person's rights, which requires users not to post any identifying documentation or sensitive financial information about another person.

The statement also places restrictions on advertisers indicating that if advertisers intend to collect personal information from users, then the advertisers must obtain consent from those users, and make it clear it is not Facebook collecting the information. The advertisers must also post a privacy policy for users to review.

In contrast, applications have much more latitude to collect information and Facebook's privacy policy does not apply to an application. Whenever a user accesses an application, the application has access to the user's information, including the user's name, friends' names, picture, gender, user ID, connections, content shared with "everyone," age, and the location of the computer or access device. The application also has access to that user's friends' information, including their names, profile pictures, genders, user IDs, and information shared with "everyone."

1.2 Facebook and minors

As mentioned earlier, Facebook does not allow children younger than the age of 13 to register for Facebook accounts. If Facebook discovers that an account belongs to a child younger than 13, it is Facebook's policy to delete that account as soon as possible. Of course, if an 11- or 12-year-old knows how to count so that the birth year shows he or she is 13, then Facebook will allow the creation of the account; not because it wants 11-year-olds, but because it has no way of determining whether an 11-year-old isn't 13.

Facebook places this prohibition on potential members because of the Children's Online Privacy Protection Act (COPPA) in the US. This law makes it clear that any website targeted at minors younger than 13 or potentially used by minors younger than 13, must request and obtain the permission of the minor's parent before the website collects any information about that child or permits access.

Facebook has a more stringent privacy policy toward minors 13 years and older as compared with the privacy policy for adults. When an adult user of Facebook indicates that "everyone" may view certain information, Facebook takes this literally and opens it to everyone on and off Facebook. That means a user's information may even show up in search engine results. For the most part, when a minor 13 years and older indicates that "everyone" may view certain information, Facebook restricts this to friends, friends of friends, and other users in the same verified school or work network.

1.3 Facebook's copyright and intellectual property infringement policies

If the owner of copyright believes a Facebook user is infringing on the owner's copyrights, then the person can fill out a Digital Millennium Copyright Act (DMCA) form online, or a hard copy notice, and send it to Facebook. If an owner of other intellectual property believes a user is infringing on the owner's intellectual property rights, the owner can fill out an automated intellectual property infringement form and send it to Facebook. Facebook then reviews the form or notice and, if everything is in order, it will remove or disable access to the impugned content and will notify the user and provide a report to the user if requested.

If that user thinks the removal or disabling of access to the impugned content was done in error, the user may file a DMCA counter-notice. If this counter-notice is in order, then Facebook will forward the notice to the alleged owner who has ten business days to file a court action, otherwise Facebook can restore the content or access to the content. Facebook also reserves the right to determine on its own if there is content that infringes on copyright or other intellectual property.

Facebook does not accept third-party reports of infringement. This means Facebook will not accept the complaint from a friend of an owner that a user is infringing the owner's copyright or intellectual property. The owner must be the one to complain.

When an advertiser infringes an owner's copyright or intellectual property, unfortunately, Facebook indicates it has no control over this infringement and is unable to remove the content or disable access. Facebook advises owners to contact the advertiser directly.

1.4 Tagging

Facebook allows users to create online photo albums and provides the opportunity to write notes about where and when the picture was taken and who is in the picture. Tagging allows the person who is putting a picture online to label each person in that picture. When a user labels another person in a photo, that photo links to the Facebook profile of that other person, and the photo becomes a picture that is viewable according to that other person's privacy settings. Tagging can also occur in posts, such as a status update, notes, and videos, viewable according to that other person's privacy settings.

Other people on Facebook can also add a tag to a picture, but it first goes to the picture's owner for authorization to add the tag. If the owner does not authorize the tag, the tag does not attach.

If a user does not want to be tagged or have the photo or other item linked to his or her profile, the user has the option to remove the tag by simply clicking the "remove tag" button. Only the user that put up the photo/item and the tagged user can remove or edit a tag. A user can set his or her notification settings to alert him or her whenever he or she is tagged.

Removing a tag from a photo disconnects any link between that photo and the user's profile and the user is no longer named as being in that photo. In contrast, removing a tag from a post such as a status update only removes the link to the user's profile and does not remove the user's name from the post. The post still stays as it was typed but without the link. This, of course, has implications for bullying.

A Facebook user can also tag someone who does not have a Facebook account by starting the tagging process and then entering that other person's email address instead. Facebook then sends an email to that other person and provides a link so he or she can view the picture. That other person can only see the pictures in which he or she is tagged and cannot see other pictures until he or she becomes a Facebook user. The other user also cannot remove the tag unless he or she creates a Facebook account using that email. This is a great feature for sharing pictures, for example, with the Grandma who does not have a Facebook profile.

1.5 Protecting yourself on Facebook

Protecting yourself on Facebook is easy and only requires a few steps and some vigilance. You can log into your Facebook account and from the account drop down menu click on privacy and user settings. You can customize these settings to your desired level of privacy. It is possible to set the settings so high that you will not show up in a general search and, if found, only your name and profile picture appear, and no person may send a message to you except a friend request. However, some vigilance is required because Facebook has a tendency to update its privacy settings and options and drop the user's settings down to Facebook's default settings, which are much more open.

Naturally, a user must be careful about the friend requests he or she accepts. It is wise that if the user does not know the requesting person, the user should not accept the friend request. It is also wise for a user to refuse friend requests from persons who have bullied him or her in the past.

If a person is harassing or bullying a user or posting items the user does not like, there are different protective steps the user can take. A user can remove tags and delete items from his or her message inbox, wall, or news feed. Removing the item from the user's wall removes it entirely and other users will not see the item.

The user can utilize his or her privacy settings to limit what the harassing person can see of the user's profile and pictures. The user can also click on the "report" button and Facebook will investigate the harassing person. It is against Facebook's policies to allow harassment and, if appropriate, Facebook can deactivate the harassing user's account.

If the harassment persists, a user can use the "block" feature in his or her privacy settings. The block feature stops all contact from the harassing person and blocks the harassing person from seeing any of the user's content. If the harassing person and the user have a mutual friend and the mutual friend posts a picture and tags the user, the harassing person cannot click on the user's name to gain access to the user's profile.

Whenever a user posts an item, the user has the choice of limiting who can see that item. There is a button with a picture of a lock. Clicking that button brings up a list of options to restrict who can see the item.

1.6 Places

No discussion of privacy on Facebook would be complete without highlighting a new geo-locating application called "Places," which was introduced in August 2010 and uses the GPS mapping functions of your smartphone to let your Facebook friends know exactly where you are, by "tagging" you, even if you're in a place you don't want others to know about.

Facebook says, "Easily share where you are, what you're doing, and the friends you're with right from your mobile. Check in and your update will appear on the Place page, your friends' News Feed, and your Wall. Tag the friends you're with so they can be part of your update.

"Appear in 'Here Now' to friends and others nearby who are also checked in. 'I'm just down the street!' Never miss another chance to connect when you happen to be at the same place at the same time. Browse status updates of friends checked in nearby."

However, if you're in a strip club, or a sexual health clinic, a job interview with a competitor, or a host of other places where you don't want anyone to know your whereabouts, Places may well be a terrible invasion of your privacy.

Demand Your dotRights (http://www.dotrights.org/), a website of the American Civil Liberties Union (ACLU) is warning people about Places. It states that the ACLU has "serious concerns about other privacy protections and controls associated with Places ... Places allows your friends to 'tag' you when they check in somewhere. But while Facebook makes it very easy to say 'yes' and allow your friends to check in for you, they make it far more difficult to say 'no,'"opening up your life to stalkers and others who know your location.

In any event, my comments respecting the geotagging of digital photographs in Chapter 8 have equal bearing on Places, Foursquare, and other geo-locating applications.

Know how to disable features that you don't want. Go into your Facebook profile, and click on "privacy settings" under the account tab. From there, click on "customize settings." Where you see the words, "Friends can check me into places," choose "disabled" from the drop down menu. If you use it, you can adjust your settings so that "check ins" are seen "only by me" if you want to see where you've been without sharing where you've been with all your "friends" on Facebook.

1.7 Improper content on Facebook

If a user comes across as offensive or has inappropriate content, or if a person sends a user offensive or inappropriate content, a user can report this content to Facebook. For example, when a user clicks the "report this photo" link, a box will open that says:

"All reports are strictly confidential."

The box also provides a menu for the user to choose the reason he or she is reporting the photo. The reasons include nudity or pornography, drug use, graphic violence, attacks on individuals or groups, and advertisement spam. A similar process occurs for reporting other items.

1.8 Facebook and the legal realm

Facebook complies with law enforcement and even publishes a handbook to assist law enforcement in understanding Facebook and learning how to request information from Facebook. However, Facebook will always respect user privacy and only provide access to the extent required by a governmental agency, and no more. Facebook prohibits convicted sex offenders from having Facebook accounts and, on receiving documentation confirming sex offender status, such as a name in a national registry, a link to an online news article, or a court document, Facebook will deactivate the sex offender's account.

For civil suits, Facebook does not permit any access to a user's account or information. This is because there are federal laws that prohibit the disclosure of user information, which includes the contents of a user's account, to any nongovernmental entity, even pursuant to a valid subpoena or court order. Facebook suggests obtaining this content through a request for the other party to produce the contents as relevant documents to the civil suit.

However, if a user leaves his or her account relatively open for others to view, then an investigator may find his or her way into that user's account to retrieve the relevant documents. Similarly, an investigator can find one of the user's friends whose account is relatively open for others to view and gain access to the user's pictures and account content from the friend's account.

Facebook has even been used by litigants to serve someone with a lawsuit. The first country to permit service by Facebook was Australia, and Canada followed a few months later when an Alberta court granted an order for service by Facebook.

1.9 Facebook safety and privacy advice

It is important for educators and parents to be aware of the different safety measures available to Facebook users and what they can do to assist a teen if he or she is being harassed or bullied. Educators and parents can report a person who is harassing a user. The "report" link is the easiest way to flag a problem.

Educators and parents should also teach teens to be careful from whom they accept friend requests and to use the "report" or "block" features if the teen becomes uncomfortable with how another person is treating him or her. The best defense by far is to talk with teens about the importance of using their privacy settings to prevent any unwanted contact before it occurs, and parents especially should work with their teens to find an appropriate level of privacy.

The comments here on privacy relate to Facebook, but generally have equal applicability on other social networking sites, even though privacy rules may differ depending on the social network you're on.

Now let's look at YouTube. It's different than Facebook. But the fact that it is the largest video-sharing platform in the world is a good reason why we should have a look at its privacy policy.

2. YouTube's Privacy Policy

Google owns YouTube, so YouTube's privacy policy is the same as Google's privacy policy. Google has five privacy principles:

1. Use information to provide our users with valuable products and services.

2. Develop products that reflect strong privacy standards and practices.

3. Make the collection of personal information transparent.

4. Give users meaningful choices to protect their privacy.

5. Be a responsible steward of the information we hold.

Google has posted three videos on YouTube explaining privacy and the information that Google collects and how that information is used. The videos are called "Google Privacy: A Look at Cookies," "Google Search Privacy: Personalized Search," and "Google Search Privacy: Plain and Simple."

Anyone can watch a YouTube video without having a YouTube account or a Google account. A person must create an account for certain activities, such as uploading videos, commenting, and flagging inappropriate or offensive content. When a person creates an account, he or she shares some personal information with YouTube including email address, password, location, zip or postal code, date of birth, and gender.

YouTube collects information about a user every time he or she uses YouTube including information about usage, groups, favorites, with whom the user communicates, frequency and size of data transfers, and any information the person displays about himself or herself. YouTube assures its users that it will not use personal information to send commercial or marketing messages without a user's consent, and will only use it for administrative purposes and to provide and improve features and functionality of YouTube.

However, YouTube does use cookies, web beacons, IP addresses, usage data, browser type and operating systems, and log file information to provide custom, personalized content and information, to monitor the effectiveness of marketing campaigns, and for aggregate metrics. Specifically, YouTube uses the DoubleClick cookie to help advertisers and publishers serve and manage ads on the site. (You can also choose to opt out of the DoubleClick cookie.)

YouTube makes some information automatically available to other YouTube users when a person signs up for an account. This includes the date the account was opened, the date the user last logged on, the user's country, and the number of videos the user has watched. Other persons will not see the user's email address and can only contact the user by leaving a message or comment on YouTube. It is up to the user whether he or she wants to provide more information.

YouTube and Google may make available applications called gadgets. Any information collected by Google when enabling a gadget is processed under Google's privacy policy, but information collected by the third-party gadget is governed by the third-party's privacy policy.

2.1 YouTube community guidelines

The community guidelines essentially tell users and potential users not to abuse the site. Basic ground rules are laid down such as no pornography or sexually explicit content, no drug use, no graphic or gratuitous violence or abuse, and no graphic videos of car accidents or dead bodies. The guidelines also requires users to respect copyright, which means users should only upload videos they made or they are authorized to use and includes not using copyrighted material in their videos. Furthermore, while free speech is important, YouTube will not tolerate anything that attacks, demeans, or discriminates against a group.

2.2 YouTube and copyright infringement

YouTube tells its users:

"Copyright infringement occurs when a copyrighted work is reproduced, distributed, performed, publicly displayed, or made into a derivative work without the permission of the copyright owner. Posting copyright-infringing content can lead to the termination of your account, and possibly monetary damages if a copyright owner decides to take legal action."

To help its users, YouTube provides a library of authorized music through AudioSwap, which users can access by logging into their account. While YouTube accepts that there may be fair use defenses for some uses, it does not want to wade into that discussion and it leaves it to the users to obtain their own legal advice.

If any person feels that their copyright has been infringed by a YouTube user, that person may file a written copyright infringement notification explaining why and how it infringes that person's copyright. YouTube makes an online complaint form available to expedite this process. Anyone whose content was removed for copyright infringement has the opportunity to submit a counter-notification.

2.3 Improper content policy on YouTube

YouTube does not tolerate improper content such as hate speech, sexual abuse of minors, harassment or cyberbullying, or impersonation. Whenever a user comes across any of this improper or offensive content, he or she should flag the videos for YouTube to review. YouTube accepts flags 24 hours per day and is often able to review and act on the flagged content within an hour of the report. Users can also report channels and comments through YouTube's "Help & Safety Tool."

If a person is harassing or cyberbullying a YouTube user, that user can block the harassing or bullying person, can control the comments that are posted to his or her channel, simply turn video comments off, or use the "Help & Safety Tool" to report the harassing or bullying person.

2.4 Protecting yourself on YouTube

There are 280 million people on YouTube. Protecting who can and cannot see information is extremely important! Users can control the information available to others and friends by customizing their account and privacy settings. Users can also control who views any videos uploaded.

There are two ways to limit who views a video. First, the user can create a private video. Once the user uploads the video, the user can change the broadcasting and sharing options to be private only. The user then has two choices, generate a unique website address that can be sent to 25 people or the user can choose to share the video with just his or her YouTube friends. The advantage of the first option is that persons without a YouTube account are still able to view the video.

Second, the user can create an unlisted video, which is a type of private video. Like the private video, an unlisted video means that only those persons who know the link to the video can view the video, including non-YouTube users, but there is the added benefit of no sharing limit.

It is always important to remember that anyone who views a user's video can share that video with other people. Therefore, it is important for a user to be careful to whom he or she sends a URL for the video or who he or she becomes friends with on YouTube.

If a user has a complaint that YouTube or Google has not conformed to its own privacy policy, complaints can be directed to Privacy Matters at Google.

2.5 YouTube and minors

YouTube requires that all users be at least 13 years of age or older before they can create a YouTube account. If YouTube discovers an account in which the user inaccurately stated his or her age, then YouTube will suspend the account. Again, if an 11- or 12-year-old can count, he or she will be able to pick a birthday that makes him or her 13 or older.

Parents and legal guardians of users may file a complaint on behalf of a child but an educator may not. If an educator is concerned, YouTube encourages him or her to contact the student's parent or guardian. However, YouTube will only accept privacy and harassment complaints directly from the user.

3. Protecting Yourself Online Generally

Protecting yourself online is all about using common sense. Provide only as much information as you are willing to share with the world and understand that the information you do share may be used by not only the site that you are using, but also by third parties linked to that website such as advertisers or application developers.

Be familiar with your computer's settings and all the settings of any online accounts you use such as email, YouTube, or Facebook. Where possible, increase any privacy settings and use customization features to reflect the level and kind of privacy you want. If you dislike websites loading cookies onto your computer, then set your computer to refuse cookies, but remember that this may impair the use of some sites or accounts, or delete your cookies from time to time. If you dislike websites recording your IP address, then it is possible to use software that generates a fake IP address.

Do not forget to look at the website for its privacy policy. This may lead you to all sorts of links and information about privacy for that site. YouTube's privacy and safety webpages are especially entertaining. You can even ask a ninja how to make your YouTube videos private! Go to *YouTube 101: Private Sharing* at www.youtube.com/watch?v=TL-S5C5U-XA.

The best tools to protect you are knowledge and common sense! There are some great websites that will provide you with information about privacy and what you can do or how you can talk to your children, students, employees, friends, and neighbors about online privacy issues.

See the following websites:

- ThatsNotCool.com
- commonsenseMedia.org
- TRUSTe.com
- VeriSign.com

3.1 Privacy breach

Your privacy has been breached or invaded or you have been defamed! Now what?

If a person posts a photo or links content to a user on Facebook that is offensive or inappropriate, the user can report the photo or content to Facebook. However, Facebook will only remove content that violates its terms of use policies and has specifically said it will not remove a photo just because a user thinks it is unflattering or does not like the way the photo looks. Therefore, to have a photo or content removed, a user should contact the creator of the posting to ask him or her to remove the content.

If an application in Facebook breaches a user's privacy, the user must remember that Facebook's privacy policy does not apply to that application. First, Facebook encourages the user to contact the application owner directly to resolve the issue. If, however, the application does not or will not resolve the user's problem, the user can then report this problem to Facebook directly. Facebook does require applications to follow certain rules regarding privacy and Facebook can choose to take action regarding a breach. But misuse of personal information by application developers or Facebook is a problem Facebook itself is getting more sensitive to, given media attention generated by the discovery of privacy breaches. For example, in October, 2010, Facebook disabled Zynga's "phrases" Facebook page for allegedly sharing personal data with data mining, Internet tracking, and advertising companies. So be very cautious about any Facebook applications as data sharing and privacy breaches can and do occur through these applications.

Similarly, YouTube provides an option to users to report or flag another person who is posting offensive or inappropriate content. YouTube will investigate complaints of breach of privacy, but cautions its users that if they are in a public place and caught on camera in passing, then YouTube is not likely to remove the video unless that user is clearly identifiable.

YouTube encourages a user to first contact the person who uploaded the privacy-breaching or defamatory content and ask him or her to remove the content. YouTube then encourages the user to use the flagging feature if the video breaches YouTube's community guidelines. If these options do not resolve the user's issue, the user can report harassment or a violation of privacy directly to YouTube. YouTube will ask for certain information including the location of the offending content in order to investigate the complaint.

When reporting a privacy violation to YouTube, the user will be asked if the violation is in relation to his or her image, voice, or full name, or his or her personal data such as email address, home address, or social security or social insurance number.

3.2 Someone is pretending to be me

If a Facebook user discovers an imposter who is pretending to be the user, it is easy to report the imposter on Facebook. Simply go to the imposter's profile and click on "report this person," check the "report this person" box, choose "fake account" as the reason, and add "impersonating me or someone else" as the report type. The user must also provide Facebook with a valid web address (URL) that leads to the imposter's profile so that Facebook can review the account.

YouTube defines impersonation as "the act of copying [another user's] exact channel layout, using a similar user name or posing as the person in comments, emails, or videos."

YouTube considers impersonation harassment and it is therefore against the community guidelines. To remove an imposter channel, use the "Help & Safety Tool" to request review for removal. To remove an imposter person, file a privacy removal request. YouTube only accepts complaints of impersonation from the impersonated and will not accept the complaint from friends or family.

However, if someone is pretending to be the user's business, YouTube does not consider this impersonation and will direct that user to the legal issues and help center portions of its website for more information.

3.3 When do you get a lawyer?

If the YouTube or Facebook user has exhausted all his or her options previously discussed, including using preventative measures such as privacy settings, deleting content or removing tags linked to that user, using the Block feature, and reporting or flagging inappropriate or offensive content, then the user still has a few more options outside of Facebook and YouTube to resolve an issue.

Facebook is a member of TRUSTe, a privacy seal provider. TRUSTe approves websites for its privacy policy and can certify websites for the US-EU and Swiss Safe Harbor program, an agreement reached between America and the EU regarding user data and privacy requirements. TRUSTe indicates that the US Federal Trade Commission has approved its certifications and programs. If a user has a problem with Facebook that the user cannot resolve with Facebook, the user can report a complaint to TRUSTe, which will then conduct an investigation into the matter.

In England, if a person who is 18 years or younger believes an adult is acting inappropriately toward him or her, he or she can submit an online report to the Child Exploitation and Online Protection Centre (CEOP).

In Canada, if a person feels that the government, a company, or an individual has invaded his or her privacy, that person can lodge a complaint with the federal or provincial Privacy Commissioner. The commissioner derives all powers to investigate and make orders through special freedom of information or protection of personal information legislation. The Commissioner and his or her office will investigate the claim and often try to mediate a settlement between the person and offending party.

Sometimes, however, this is not the route a person may prefer to take if the invasion of privacy or defamation is of such a serious nature that it warrants obtaining legal advice. Some lawyers will offer a free first interview session to discuss your rights and whether a privacy or defamation issue warrants legal action.

One of the most famous stories of invasion of privacy involves the "Star Wars Kid." This video was filmed in 2002 and in 2003 became a viral video sensation. The original video has almost 18 million views on YouTube and others estimate the video has been viewed at least 1 billion times. There are also numerous spoof videos and references in such shows as *South Park* and *American Dad*.

The "Star Wars Kid" and his parents sued the boy who posted the video and his parents claiming that the child "had to endure, and still endures today, harassment and derision from his high school mates and the public at large" and "will be under psychiatric care for an indefinite amount of time." The case did not proceed to trial and settled out of court for $250,000.

The "Star Wars Kid" has apparently moved past this embarrassing and mentally damaging portion of his life, is pursuing a law degree at McGill University, and is the president of a conservation society for the cultural heritage of Trois-Riviéres. There is life after a privacy violation.

Lawyers are expensive though, and mainstream media are constantly looking for stories on the use and misuse of social media, particularly in relation to Facebook and YouTube.

You might want to bring your complaint to the court of public opinion through media interviews for arguably swifter action. Or, consider recording a YouTube video about it.

12
RESOURCES AND INTERESTING FACTS

When you're researching and writing a book on something as new as "online reputation management," there's a lot of information that just doesn't fit quite anywhere else. It's the square peg that doesn't quite go in the round hole, but is important nonetheless. This chapter is a collection of interesting tidbits, miscellany, and other information that you'll hopefully find of interest, including resources that you can use for more information.

1. Never Underestimate the Power of Social Networks and Social Contagion

Although this book has looked at the issue of online social networks, almost as important are the offline social networks we belong to, which may comprise our family, our circle of friends, our colleagues, and others who we interact with in our communities. The offline social networks that we create and belong to may have a greater influence than we might think.

Nicholas Christakis from Harvard University and James Fowler of the University of California in San Diego published *Connected: The Surprising Power of Our Social Networks and How They Shape Our Lives*. The book isn't so much about Facebook and online social networking as it is about offline networking, and how the company we keep and the friends we have affect our lives and behavior more than we might think.

Christakis spoke at a conference at Oxford in November 2009 and made the following points:

- If a friend in your network of friends gains weight, someone else in that circle is likely to as well. If a friend in the same network of friends loses weight, someone else in that circle is likely to lose weight as well.

- If someone in the room is filled with joy and happiness, it will spread to others like a contagion.

- If someone in the room quits smoking, chances are others will too.

Our actions may be determined by free will but they might also be influenced by something called "social contagion."

For example, if your friends are overweight, you and your friends may be more likely to go out for junk food together. You have a greater propensity to become overweight by the company you keep. However, you also might become overweight by simply knowing people who are overweight. The herding instinct of the crowd influences our behavior extraordinarily; people affect each other regarding matters that they wouldn't expect.

In another study, "Breaking up Is Hard to Do, Unless Everyone Else Is Doing It Too: Social Network Effects on Divorce in a Longitudinal Sample Followed for 32 Years" (coauthored by Rose McDermott of Brown University, Fowler, and Christakis), the authors examined divorce within social networks, as McDermott had seen divorce spread "like a contagion" among her own circle of friends. Her study concluded that divorce was indeed, contagious. Based on a community which had been a "study group" for a variety of ailments since the 1940s, people with a friend in that community who had divorced were 147 percent more likely to be divorced themselves within five years. People with a divorced brother or sister were 22 percent more likely to divorce within five years than those without a divorced sibling. People with a divorced coworker were 55 percent more likely to divorce within five years than those with a non-divorced coworker.

Implied in the study is that among a person's "network of friends," he or she didn't have to get divorced to pass along the "divorce bug." The person could simply be a carrier. "If you know someone who gets divorced, it might change your attitude as to whether it's acceptable, which you may then transmit to other friends who may not know the first person," said Dr. Fowler to *The Globe and Mail* ("Keeping up with the Ex-Joneses," by Sarah Hampson, July 15, 2010), who coauthored the study with McDermott. "This is really about norms. Social networks influence virtually everything about love, sex, and relationships."

Social networks have "such a strong effect that not only do we copy our friends, but we end up copying our friends' friends and even our friends' friends' friends," Fowler said in *The Globe and Mail*. "If I don't know anything about you but I know your friend's friend has divorced, I can be good at predicting whether you will get divorced."

McDermott said in the same piece, "If you get divorced and think you'll be alone, you might be less likely to do it. But if you have divorced, single friends, that makes it easier because you have a network."

2. Every Cell Phone Is a Camera and Every Microphone Is Live

How can anyone forget the performance of American swimmer Michael Phelps at the 2008 Summer Olympics in Beijing? He won eight gold medals. In the 2004 Athens Olympics four years earlier, he won six gold and two bronze medals. Mark Spitz, the 1972 swimming sensation (who won 7 gold medals at the 1972 Munich Olympics), said about Phelps, "He's maybe the greatest athlete ... to walk the planet."

Phelps' star (and his value) rose dramatically after Beijing, with a name, a face, and a reputation known around the world. He received money from endorsements from Visa and other corporations after the Athens Olympics, but a nanosecond after the Beijing Olympics, the endorsement money flooded to Phelps like bees to honey. Phelps' agent, Peter Carlisle, said, "What is the value of eight gold [medals] in Beijing before a prime-time audience in the US? I'd say $100 million over the course of his lifetime."

Now recall Michael Phelps went to a party at the University of South Carolina in the fall of 2008. He did what lots of 23-year-olds do at parties — he smoked marijuana from a bong. However, someone with a camera (or a camera in a cell phone), took his picture with his face buried in the bong. Unlike Bill Clinton's admission that he never inhaled marijuana while at university, a picture says a thousand words.

The picture ended up on the cover of the London tabloid *News of the World* in January 2009 with the headline "PHELPS GOES BONG."

USA Swimming, the governing body for amateur swimming in the United States, suspended him for three months over the incident. It said in a statement:

"This is not a situation where any anti-doping rule was violated, but we decided to send a strong message to Michael because he disappointed so many people, particularly the hundreds of thousands of USA Swimming member kids who look up to him as a role model and a hero."

The US Olympic Committee said it was "disappointed in the behavior recently exhibited by Michael Phelps. Michael is a role model, and he is well aware of the responsibilities and accountability that come with setting a positive example for others, particularly young people. In this instance, regrettably, he failed to fulfill those responsibilities."

Phelps issued the following statement:

"I engaged in behavior which was regrettable and demonstrated bad judgment. I'm 23 years old and despite the successes I've had in the pool, I acted in a youthful and inappropriate way, not in a manner people have come to expect from me. For this, I am sorry. I promise my fans and the public it will not happen again."

As for endorsements, they didn't dry up. But if you're a lawyer or a business agent for Nike, Speedo, Omega, or Visa in charge of negotiating Phelps' endorsement contracts, you're going to ask this question: Is the Olympian still worth all that money after the bong incident than before it?

Kellogg's didn't think so. It dropped him as a sponsor for Kellogg's Corn Flakes, stating:

"We originally built the relationship with Michael, as well as the other Olympic athletes, to support our association with the US Olympic team. Michael's most recent behavior is not consistent with the image of Kellogg's. His contract expires at the end of February and we have made a decision not to extend his contract."

If you're a celebrity and a role model like Phelps (or soon expect to be), everything you do will be seen by others and scrutinized. Everything. Expect both amateur and professional paparazzi to take your picture whenever and wherever they can. You're in the public domain now. You may even be a role model for kids. Those pictures of you "letting loose" for a night can be sold to newspapers and magazines for tens of thousands of dollars, so you have to protect your digital image from those who would seek to embarrass you or otherwise profit from a compromising photograph.

In 1973, I was in Grade 11 at St. Michaels University School in Victoria, which was at that time an all-boys school. (Think of Hogwarts with lots of Rugby but no magic and you'll get a sense of the place back then!) In June of that year, we were looking to do some harmless "end of school" pranks, rather like what some engineering students do to Volkswagens suspended from bridges when they graduate — except we didn't have the engineering skills, the Volkswagen, or the bridge!

One of the boys brought to school a wireless microphone, the size of a pen. When activated, you could pick up conversations from the microphone on an FM radio nearby. No big technological breakthrough these days, but in those days, it was amazing.

One of the Grade 12 students saw the microphone and suggested we hide the "bug" in the room where the teachers were holding their end-of-year staff meeting to decide on all the school awards.

The bug was planted in an envelope, and addressed to a fictitious person, and put in the staff room. Word got around that the staff meeting was being broadcast on 88.3 FM. Every boarding student had their radios on and their antenna's pointed skyward out the windows of the dorms. Every student of driving age had their cars parked near the staff room for the best reception. It was surreal, because we discovered who was, and who was not going to receive the school's coveted cup.

Surprisingly, a few teachers who were on "hall patrol" that day instead of at the staff meeting had probably heard the broadcast. However, the microphone was never found and there was no recording of the meeting — no student was ever caught. The lesson here is to warn parents, teachers, and business persons this: if a 16- and 17-year-old can plant a bug in a staff meeting in 1973, imagine what can happen in the second decade of the twenty-first century. You never know when you'll be "live."

Public figures are often overheard saying something they shouldn't say near a live microphone. US figure skater, Nancy Kerrigan, was attacked in the knee by an assailant in 1994. The attack happened so Kerrigan couldn't compete against Tonya Harding in the US Skating Championship that year. After the attack, and her return to skating, she had the sympathy of all America, including the Walt Disney Company, who featured her on a Disney float at a Disneyland parade. As she smiled at the crowd, she said, "This is dumb. I hate it. This is the most corniest thing I have ever done."

Regrettably, she was within earshot of a live microphone, which picked up the offhand remark. Needless to say, Disney ended its relationship with Kerrigan.

You'd think actor and director Mel Gibson would have learned from a racist slur made to a police officer who was arresting him for drunk driving in 2006, but in 2010, he was recorded on voice mail saying awful and degrading things to Oksana Grigorieva, his ex-girlfriend and the mother of one of his children.

During the cold war, US President Ronald Reagan during a sound check before a radio broadcast, made these comments, "My fellow Americans, I'm pleased to tell you today that I've signed legislation that will outlaw Russia forever. We begin bombing in five minutes."

In 2010, then UK Prime Minister Gordon Brown was caught on a live microphone describing a female voter as a "bigoted woman."

In 2005, French President Jacques Chirac, also didn't realize his microphone was live when he told someone in a private conversation during the bid for the 2012 Olympic Games, about rival bidder, London, "The only thing they have ever done for European agriculture is mad cow disease. One cannot trust people whose cuisine is so bad. After Finland, it is the country with the worst food."

The message is loud and clear. Whether you're the leader of a great nation; the featured celebrity in a parade; a school principal at morning assembly; or a corporate lawyer at an annual general meeting of shareholders, assume there's a microphone nearby and that it's live.

3. All Facebook

One of the more interesting websites I've found is All Facebook — The Unofficial Facebook Resource. You can subscribe to daily emails by following the links on AllFacebook.com's webpage. If you want to be up-to-date with stories about what new "explosive" applications

Facebook is developing or launching (or a third-party provider is launching); Facebook's never-ending privacy problems; lawsuits involving Facebook users and users of social media; breaking news about social media in general and Facebook in particular; the profoundly stupid things people do on social media; and, of course, unsubstantiated gossip about Facebook and other social media platforms, this is the site for you.

If I had to pick 300 words of the most interesting things I've seen on All Facebook, it's the scams that the site has reported on and exposed. As email has become a target for phishers, spammers, and other scams, so too has Facebook. Here is All Facebook's list of the top scams:

- **IQ quiz advertisement:** Facebook advertisements normally appear on the right hand side of any page you navigate to. But you really have to be careful navigating to any of them, especially IQ Quiz type ads. One in particular, called the 10 Mind Quiz, directs people to a website where they are asked questions relating to their IQ (the questions were not difficult). In order to get the answers, people are asked to provide their telephone numbers. It's reported that if they provide their phone number as the site requests, their telephone bill will be charged close to $10 per week.

  The rule here is not to enter things like your telephone number, your birthday, any credit card number, or other personal information in websites that pop up in Facebook in response to a quiz, or for that matter, any websites that you don't know well enough to trust. If you're asked to provide an email address, you might think of creating a "dummy" address on Gmail, Yahoo!, or Hotmail that is not a main address or even a secondary address and which you can eliminate at any time if providing the address has triggered spam. I have two Gmail accounts for that very purpose. If they get spam, I can dump them.

- **C VVHO HAS VIEVVED YOU:** All Facebook commented on this scam, and I admit receiving something from a friend that thought this was a fabulous application. My "friend" of course didn't send it. If you see the spelling, it looks like "see who has viewed you" but you'll note the W's have been replaced by two Vs.

  As attractive as it may be to find out who may have viewed your Facebook profile, your photographs or any other part of your Facebook page ("creeped" you, as they say), over 40,000 people have downloaded this phishing application as of the date of writing. It works in this way. A "friend" makes a suggestion for you to access the C VVHO HAS VIEVVED YOU website. When you do, you are asked to copy and paste your URL into your browser. Then a popup ad appears so you can invite friends. If you catch on too late and select "none" or "cancel," all your Facebook friends will be sent the same invitation. You have to get out of the application within three or four seconds or invites are automatically sent to all your "friends."

As of the date of writing, there is no application that allows Facebook users to see who has viewed their profiles, photographs, or other information. Facebook does not provide an application that allows users to track profile views or statistics on views of any user content. "C VVHO HAS VIEVVED YOU" is a phishing site and a scam.

- **Please send money:** Another scam you may have encountered is this one. You're on Facebook and a "friend" of yours sends an instant message that he or she is in another country. The person claims to have been robbed and he or she doesn't have money or credit cards to get home. How your friend has somehow found a computer, and paid for it in an Internet cafe is a question you might want to ask. Why the person wouldn't phone his or her family members "collect" is another good question; that is, why would the person instant message you when he or she has family who might accept collect telephone calls from a stranded family member?

    In any event, it's a scam where you're asked to send your friend money through Western Union. Clearly, someone has compromised another person's Facebook account and is going through the friend's list to attempt to have someone send the scammer money.

- **Posted links:** Another phishing scam consists of a Facebook friend sending a message that says "hey got a great picture of you here" and directs the person to an URL.

- **Help keep Facebook free:** I've received this one. A message is sent to a Facebook user from a group suggesting Facebook will not be free anymore and that people will be charged for using

Facebook. The message invites users to sign a petition against it. The message says, "Facebook is pushing for pay-per-user again. We successfully stopped them before, and we can do it again! … Visit our partner's website and submit your email to sign the petition now! Tell everybody; only by working together can we beat this." If you go to the "partner's website," you are sent to a business site where the owner receives money per click.

It all comes back to exercising a healthy degree of skepticism regarding anything posted on Facebook that encourages you to go to a website and provide information; whether that information is your email address, phone number, or some other information that is personal to you and could be compromising if it found its way into someone else's hands. Don't give out any information to people, organizations, or businesses you don't know.

Other scams that have made it into the news include the story of an 18-year-old boy from Wisconsin who apparently used a dummy Facebook account to pose as a woman in order to lure high school boys to send him naked pictures of themselves. He then blackmailed the boys who sent the pictures "to coerce them into having sex acts with him." Sextortion is a serious problem and discussed in more detail in Chapter 7.

3.1 Other resources

There are other resources besides All Facebook, such as blogs or websites. The following outlines a few resources:

- CyberInquirer is a good resource to stay on top of developments regarding Internet use in general and online social networking in particular.

- Pew Internet has been mentioned throughout this book. The Internet & American Life Project studies the effect of Internet and online technology on the lives of Americans, and the various studies undertaken by Pew have applicability not just to Americans, but to all persons who use Internet technology in their work and their day-to-day activities. Pew Internet & American Life Project is an invaluable resource, and one of seven projects carried out by the Pew Research Center. The other projects studied by Pew researchers include The Pew Forum on Religion & Public Life, Pew Global Attitudes

Project, Pew Social & Demographic Trends, Project for Excellence in Journalism, Pew Research Center for the People & the Press, and the Pew Hispanic Center. (Pew Research Center, by the way, is funded through trusts established by heirs to the Sun Oil fortune.)

• TED.com is an essential resource for an inquisitive mind looking for new trends, new ideas, or interesting perspectives on old ideas. TED is a nonprofit entity devoted to "ideas worth spreading." TED brings together some of the world's most interesting thinkers and doers, who are asked to give the "talk of their lives" in no more than 18 minutes. These talks are recorded for playback on TED's website. There are more than a thousand "Tedcasts" on a multitude of topics, but you can see presentations about how the Internet in general and online communication in particular is changing how people communicate, how they make decisions, and even how they report news.

• Failbook is one blog that will keep you on top of the more stupid things posted to Facebook. Failbook finds (or is sent) the dumbest status updates; dumb being, in this case, funny.

• Web 2.0 Suicide Machine was launched in 2010 to enable Facebook users to metaphorically kill themselves online by deleting all of their information from social networking sites. The gist of Web 2.0 Suicide Machine is that the information you input within the program will run another program that erases your profile and deletes all of your friends from your status updates and other messages one by one, subsequently changing your user name and password so that you can't log back in.

4. Don't Make Death Threats on Facebook

The Vancouver Sun reported on April 23, 2010 that the RCMP and the Vancouver police were investigating death threats against Canadian politician Ujjal Dosanjh. Dosanjh, a former Premier of British Columbia and a member of the Federal Parliament in Ottawa, is of the Sikh faith and was born in India. Someone created a Facebook group page called "Ujjal Dosanjh is a Sikh traitor." This was a description of the page:

"Ujjal Dosanjh is a Canadian member of Parliament who used his Sikh roots to get elected in Vancouver but then betrayed his own people. He totally approves of India's genocide of the Sikhs and calls anyone who demands justice for the Sikh's a terrorist ... [he is a] scumbag traitor and an insult to the Sikh religion. All content is public."

At the time this site was taken down by Facebook it had 183 members and one of the posts called Ujjal Dosanjh a "traitor who should be shot." Police are continuing to investigate the authors of the fan page and the death threat post.

5. A Different Approach: A Wild Reputation Can Be Good for a Company!

Chip Conley is the founder and CEO of Joie de Vivre Hospitality. He has an MBA from Stanford University and acquired his first hotel at age 26. As of 2010, Joie de Vivre has annual revenues of more than $240 million and employs more than 3,000 employees in its many hotels.

Conley did something that most CEOs might not do. He attended the Burning Man Project in northern Nevada. Lots of pictures were taken of Conley including one where he wore a tutu and another where he wore a sarong. He posted the pictures to Facebook.

This triggered some personal naval gazing on his part in an article that he wrote for *BNET News* in October 2009. In it he said, "I'm just not a blazer kind of guy. I consider myself a rebel. My first book — preaches the value of authenticity in business, of being true to yourself. So a few pictures on my Facebook page that show me having a good time? I honestly didn't give it a second thought."

However, some of his staff were concerned about his image, his personal soul searching comments on Twitter, and whether a double standard was being created where everyone in the company had to act in a particular way — except him.

His human resources chief suggested that the shirtless pictures of the CEO be taken off Facebook. However, Conley said in the piece, "my reaction was swift: 'screw that'! I said, People who don't like it can go work at the Marriott ... I still plan to stick to my guns, practice what I preach about authenticity, and keep the photos on my Facebook page."

Here's information that may well run against the grain of the rest of this book. Crafting and sculpting a reputation that is "not you" and "not true to your ideals" may not be good for your business and may in fact damage your reputation if your reputation is being avant-garde, off the wall, or otherwise nonconforming and iconoclastic. It just depends on you and your business. In other words, not all tattoos should be removed, even the digital ones. It just depends on the circumstances and involves common sense.

Here's what Conley said about that: "Sometimes it's straightforward — employees can't, for example, write about trade secrets — but other times, it's not. What if pictures emerge of a desk host drinking from a beer bong at a football game, or decked out in an S&M getup at an underground club? I'd have no problem with that, although I know plenty of CEOs who would. To me, that's an employee's private life. Take it a step farther — the employee is shown stealing municipal signs, for instance — and I would have a problem with it. Even worse would be if that employee is wearing a Joie de Vivre shirt. In other words, it's a case-by-case basis."

6. You Can Only Have 150 Friends

A study by Oxford University Professor of Anthropology, Robin Dunbar, indicates that, notwithstanding the propensity to collect several hundred (or even thousand) friends on Facebook and other social networking sites, the human mind is capable of handling no more than 150 relationships at a time. Dunbar's research on the part of the brain that deals with thinking and language concluded that the brain "can't deal with more than 150 friends"; friends defined as a person who cares enough about the person to contact him or her at least once a year. This has been coined in anthropological circles as "Dunbar's number."

Dunbar believes the upper limit of names we can put to faces is between 1,500 to 2,000, meaning that if you have 2,500 friends on your Facebook site, you probably can't name 500 of them. The brain just can't meaningfully do it.

7. Barack Obama Says, "Watch What You Say on Facebook"

US President Barack Obama spoke in September 2009 to Grade 9 Students at Wakefield High School in Arlington, Virginia about Facebook. A student asked what he had to do to become President. "When you're young," said the President, "you make mistakes and you do some stupid stuff." He also said, "I want everybody here to be careful about what you post on Facebook, because in the YouTube age whatever you do will be pulled up again later somewhere in your life."

Concerning Facebook postings negatively affecting job applications, the President said, "I've been hearing a lot about young people who are posting stuff on Facebook and then they suddenly go and apply for a job," in reference to employers' practice for looking for applicants' Facebook pages.

8. Top Ten Mistakes Lawyers Make with Social Media

Doug Cornelius blogs on compliance and business ethics on his site, Compliance Building. The following information comes from Cornelius' blog post: "Top Ten Mistakes Lawyers Make with Social Media" (August 1, 2009). It is reproduced here (with permission) because many of the same points are applicable to other businesses.

Lawyers and law firms are rapidly adopting social media to market themselves and connect with peers. These are new tools. We are all trying to figure out how to use them. Just to make it more difficult, the tools themselves are rapidly evolving as we are learning how to use them.

Some lawyers are doing a great job using them. Some are doing a terrible job.

I thought I would share my thoughts on the mistakes I see.

10. **Blocking access.** Social media provides a rich source of information about clients, potential clients, opposing counsel, witnesses, and other parties. It's easy to get around the block with a mobile device or home access. Blocking is just an annoyance. It's not an effective policy.

9. **Failing to have a social media policy.** People in your law firm are using social media. They may only be using it for personal purposes. But if they identify your firm as their employer, what they do has an effect on the image of your firm.

8. **Ignoring Facebook as a recruiting tool.** "You do better fishin' where the fish are." Many summer associates are creating groups on their own. Your firm would be better off if they administered the group.

7. **Not giving authorship to blog posts.** The attorneys writing the story should get credit for the story. This gives attorneys an extra incentive to contribute and showcases their skills.

6. **Not linking.** A blog is much more useful to its readers and its authors if it links to other relevant information. There is no reason not to link to primary source material like statutes and regulations online. Link to other news sources, websites, and blogs. Yes people will leave your site through those links. But they are more likely to come back if your site is the better source of information.

5. **Failing to understand ethical limitations.** The bar regulators have barely dealt with web 1.0, never mind the additional issues around web 2.0. Keep in mind that most social media activities can be considered advertising.

4. **Abandoning without notice.** Nothing lasts forever. If you started a blog and are not posting any more, put a post saying you've stopped or are on hiatus.

3. **Failing to leverage LinkedIn.** You should have a profile in LinkedIn that has at least as much information as the bio on your firm's site. You should also be leveraging LinkedIn to stay up to date with the movement of your clients and former client contacts. LinkedIn is a great source of information for CRM (customer relationship management) systems.

2. **Posting information about clients.** As with any advertising, make sure you get written consent from clients before posting any information about your work with them.

1. **Not using social media.** The biggest mistake most lawyers are making with social media is not using these tools. They are here to stay. Get used to it.